THE ANGLO-SAXONS

Saxons plundering a Roman villa

METHUEN'S Ⓜ OUTLINES

THE
ANGLO-SAXONS

by
R. R. SELLMAN

Maps and diagrams by the Author
and illustrations by
KENNETH ODY

METHUEN & CO LTD
36 ESSEX STREET · STRAND · LONDON WC2

First published 1959

© 1959 by R. R. Sellman

Printed in Great Britain by

W. & J. Mackay & Co Ltd, Chatham

Catalogue No. 6145/U

CONTENTS

Front of Northumbrian whale-ivory cabinet of the Conversion period. Left, pagan scene of Wayland the Smith. Right, the Magi visit the infant Jesus. The main runic inscription describes the stranding of the whale; the four small runes form the word 'Magi'.

THE two centuries between the withdrawal of Roman troops and government from these islands and the coming of Christian missionaries to the English have long been regarded as the 'dark age' of British history. They were 'dark' in two senses: they saw the decay and collapse of a civilisation, and hardly any record remains of the details, or even the outline, of events. About 400 A.D. Britain is still a Roman province, with towns and villas, roads, forts, and troops. Two centuries later nearly all of what had been its most civilised area is in the hands of barbarians from the continent, and amidst its ruins an alien people have established an utterly different way of life.

Of the intervening period we know tantalisingly little. The English at this time did not write at all, apart from a few short runic inscriptions: and the Britons or Welsh, whose Christian clergy kept the art of writing from Roman times, were not interested in recording a national disaster. Those who could have given us the facts either kept silent or confined themselves to violent sermons against the sins of their countrymen. On the English side, tales of the Conquest were told round the firesides, but were not written down till centuries later. The 'Anglo-Saxon Chronicle', compiled in King Alfred's time, purports to give some outline of events, and doubtless much of its story is based on fact: but its dates, and even its clear statements, need to be supported by other evidence before we can accept them. Continental writers of the time hardly mention Britain, and when they do it is plain that what was happening there was more a mystery to them than it is now to us.

The story of these two centuries must be pieced together mainly from archaeological evidence, and even here big gaps remain. The timber or mud and thatch of the early English settlements has perished so thoroughly that we have the greatest difficulty in tracing them for excavation. The first comers struck no coins, for the most part made only the crudest pottery, and left practically no inscriptions. As with many earlier peoples, their graves are almost the only evidence for their equipment, their physical type, and the areas they settled. Fortunately for the archaeologist the first English, as pagans, mostly buried with the dead those objects which were precious or useful to the living, whether the body was cremated or interred in the ordinary way. Such finds help us to map the routes and extent of early settlement; but it is certain that many of their unmarked cemeteries have not yet been discovered, and that some, destroyed by quarrying, building, or erosion, never will be. Dating, without the coins and mass-produced pottery which are the archaeologist's stand-by on Roman sites, is not easy. It is never safe to assume that an article found in a grave,

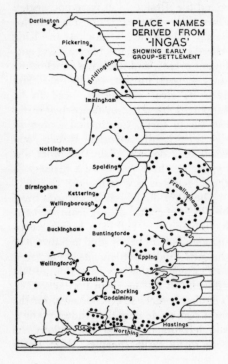

PLACE - NAMES DERIVED FROM '-INGAS' SHOWING EARLY GROUP-SETTLEMENT

even if it can itself be dated, gives the time of burial. Many such may have been heirlooms which had been passed on for generations. Only by patiently gathering and comparing evidence from as many sites as possible can a reasonably reliable picture be built up, and this work will go on for many years yet.

Something can be gathered from place-names. Those which contain an obvious name of a heathen god or word for a place of worship can be safely taken to show settlement before the arrival of Christianity. Others whose early forms show them to have ended in '-ingas' (e.g. Hastings) originally meant a group of people rather than a place, and may be taken to prove early settlement by the followers or kinsmen of someone whose name forms the first part of the compound.

On the British side the evidence is also very limited. A few crude coins were struck in post-Roman times, and a few tombstones or memorials with inscriptions in dubious Latin remain. Beyond these there are only the writings of Gildas and Nennius, and some Welsh sagas, to throw a dim and uncertain light on the period.

THE ENGLISH PEOPLES

It is this very uncertainty that makes the task of reconstruction so interesting. Each new piece of evidence as it appears adds another fragment to the immense jig-saw puzzle, supporting or disproving previous guesses. The whole picture will probably never be quite completed, for some pieces are lost for ever; but year by year the outlines are becoming clearer. About some things we are less certain than the historians of fifty years ago,

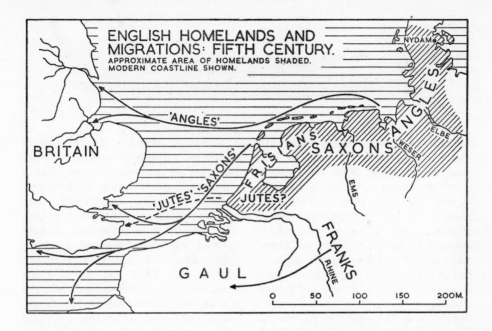

ENGLISH HOMELANDS AND MIGRATIONS: FIFTH CENTURY.
APPROXIMATE AREA OF HOMELANDS SHADED.
MODERN COASTLINE SHOWN.

because we know more. For example, the old clear-cut distinction between Angles, Saxons, and Jutes has had to be given up. Whatever their original differences, it now seems that in England the Angles and Saxons were a compound people better described by the term 'Anglo-Saxon'. Variations of dialect and fashion are so slight here that they may well have developed on the spot. The Romans, and later the Celts of Cornwall, Wales, and the North, called them all 'Saxons' without distinction, while the 'Saxons' of Southern England called themselves and their language 'Angles' and 'English'. The northern 'Angles' likewise, on occasion called England 'Saxony', while describing the southerners as 'Angles'. The fact remains that kingdoms called after the Middle and East Angles, and the West,

South, East, and perhaps Middle Saxons, came into being: but it may be that these names represent a memory of an older distinction which no longer had much meaning.

The 'Jutes' are a different matter, but even here ideas have suffered revision. It is now clear that they did not come, as Bede (see page 50) imagined, direct from Jutland. Indeed, we can hardly be sure that the invaders of Kent were Jutes at all: they never used the name for themselves or their settlements. They differed from the Anglo-Saxons in many ways which suggest that they came from Frisia and the lower Rhine, though some at least of these differences may have developed in England from close contacts between Kent and Frankish Gaul. Oddly enough, it is only in the later

3

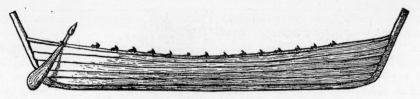

Nydam boat

Kentish colony in southern Hampshire that we find the word 'Jute' in local place-names. While Kent shows much that is not found in the rest of England, its graves have also yielded brooches and pottery formerly thought to be 'Angle' or 'Saxon', and similar objects once held to belong exclusively to 'Angle' or 'Saxon' territory are now being found in both.

The English, in fact, were a mixed race before they came to Britain, and the circumstances of migration mixed them still further. With the small rowing-boats of the time there could be no moving whole tribes or nations *en masse* to preserve their identity in the new land. Instead there was a gradual infiltration of small parties, beginning with warrior-adventurers and followed by farmers and families, seizing land where they could and in due course building up a new society which owed little to their continental origins and much to the geography of their new country.

Some of the English had been raiding Britain and the opposite coasts of Gaul for at least a century and a half before any of them settled there. Their own land, like that of the Vikings later on, was poor and over-peopled. Much of it along the North German coast was actually sinking into the sea, as we learn from the mound-settlements which they raised repeatedly to keep them above the water. To them, the Roman provinces were at first simply

a source of portable plunder. While troops still manned the massive harbour-fortresses of south-east Britain, and a naval patrol operated, they could do little more than surprise unprotected places and hope to get away with loot and captives before they were cornered. At least once in the fourth century, however, they managed a large-scale attack in concert with Picts and Irish, which submerged the defences and left the province for a short while at their mercy. But Rome, though weakening, could still spare troops to restore the situation. There could be no settlement on any scale till the way was clear to bring in wives and families.

BOATS AND EQUIPMENT

Fortunately we have a very clear idea of the boats which the English used in their raids and migrations, since examples have been found in the peat bogs of Slesvig. The most complete of these, known from its place of discovery as the Nydam boat, is an open rowing vessel some 77 feet long and under 11 feet wide. It is clinker-built, of wide oak planks extending its full length, and the sides are low enough for the oars to be worked over the gunwales (instead of through holes in the side, as in Viking ships). The peculiar one-sided rowlocks roped to the gunwales did not allow the vessel to be

4

backed, and the keel was too weak to take a mast even if—as is most unlikely—a sail could have been used without overturning the boat. In the open sea these craft must have been highly unpleasant and dangerous: without ballast they were unsteady, and with it they were so low in the water that they risked being swamped. Steering, as in all ships until the twelfth century, was by paddle and tiller in the stern.

These boats were the ancestors, but certainly not the equivalents, of the later Viking ships* with which they are sometimes confused. (It is not long since the Danes marked the fifteen-hundredth anniversary of the supposed landing of Hengist in 449 by crossing the North Sea in a vessel modelled on those of four centuries later!) In sea-worthiness and manoeuvrability there was no comparison, and even crossing the Straits of Dover in such craft must have been chancy. Yet by the later fourth century they were ranging right up to the coast of Yorkshire, as the line of Roman blockhouse signal-stations

*See *The Vikings*, by R. R. Sellman.

with their slaughtered garrisons bears witness.

For some religious or superstitious reason, perhaps sacrifice, the Slesvig boats had been deliberately broken. So too had the war-equipment found with them—thrusting-spears with ashwood shafts over 8 feet long and iron heads, lighter throwing spears, bows, and the swords and armour imported at this period from Roman workshops in the Rhineland. With the fifth-century collapse of the Roman Empire, its armourers mostly went out of business; and the actual invaders of Britain must have found it hard to get the mail coats, helmets, and longswords which were beyond the scope of their own primitive smiths. Shields were round, made of wooden planks and often covered with hide, with a metal boss in the centre covering the handgrip and iron binding at the edge.

Besides boats and weapons, humans also were sacrificed. Corpses have been found preserved in the peat, wearing the clothing of the period—large woollen cloaks sometimes rainproofed with

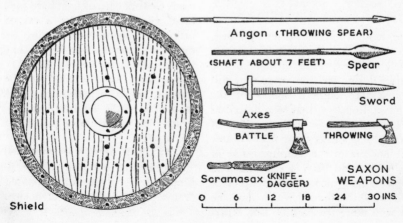

Angon (THROWING SPEAR)

(SHAFT ABOUT 7 FEET) Spear

Sword

Axes

BATTLE   THROWING

Scramasax (KNIFE-DAGGER)   SAXON WEAPONS

Shield

0   6   12   18   24   30 INS.

5

A mail byrnie

How the rings of mail interlocked

leather, loose trousers held up by a belt, and leg-wrappings like puttees.

We know very little of our remote ancestors during the time when they still inhabited the southern shores of the North Sea. Roman writers who described the Germans were generally speaking of an earlier time and of those tribes nearer to the borders of the Empire. Some of them, wishing to draw a contrast with their own countrymen, produced a picture of the 'noble barbarian' which must be taken with more than a little salt. Apart

from this, the forefathers of the English were not typical of the German peoples who invaded the Empire in the fifth century. Many of them had moved westwards quite recently from the Jutland peninsula, and very few had enough peaceful contact with Roman life to discover anything of the benefits and conveniences of civilisation. Those who later crossed the Rhine to conquer Gaul had learned much from service as auxiliaries in the provincial armies, and from trade: they were also better organised in large tribal units, able when the time came to conquer and enjoy areas of Roman territory which were still something of a going concern. But the Anglo-Saxons, already mixed and uprooted, had neither the vessels nor the numbers and organisation to make a quick and sweeping conquest. Nor, if this had been possible, would they have known what to do with a civilised land once they had won it.

The picture which emerges from excavation, in Germany and in the earliest settlements in England, is of a people hardened by a fierce struggle with nature, ready to work hard or fight hard for a bare existence, dominated by a savage and primitive religion, and having for the most part little thought for anything but their immediate needs. It was such people who, from the middle of the fifth century, began to penetrate into Britain in search of the land and living-space which their own country lacked.

THE END OF ROMAN BRITAIN*

The decline and fall of the Roman Empire is an outstanding example of a drama repeated throughout ancient his-

*See also *Roman Britain*, by R. R. Sellman.

tory, from China to Peru. Civilisations rise, powerful governments are established, and in their days of vigour empires are built by organisation and discipline. For a time they flourish in prosperity and peace, and then something goes wrong. The wider and wealthier the empire, the more its government tends to become oppressive and its rich men to become richer at the expense of the rest. Energies wither, armies become mercenaries suppressing rather than protecting the population, and meanwhile wealth attracts the greed of warlike barbarians hovering round the frontiers. Sooner or later there is a crash: the barbarians break in, often meeting little opposition from the mass of people who have lost faith in a government which has kept them cowed and disarmed. Civilisation itself may collapse, or it may survive, shaken, under new masters.

By the early fifth century the western Roman Empire reached this point of collapse. Its armies, now mainly recruited from the barbarians themselves or from the lowest grade of peasantry, had lost the discipline which had brought mastery in the great days of the legions. They were as likely to fight against the emperor as for him, and frequently left the frontiers undefended to start a civil war in the interests of their own commander. Even such great natural barriers as the Rhine, the Danube, and the Alps, strengthened by forts and military roads, could no longer be securely held against the mounting pressure without. With Rome itself in danger, the remote British province could no longer be governed or protected. We know that many of the best troops had already been withdrawn in 383,

when their commander Maximus took them across to Gaul in the hope of making himself emperor, and it is unlikely that most of them ever returned. More went in 402, to meet the Gothic invasion, and of those remaining yet more crossed the Channel under another usurping general soon afterwards. In 410 the unprotected Britons appealed to the emperor Honorius for help; but Rome itself was on the point of sack by the Goths, and all he could do was to instruct the British tribal authorities to organise their own government and defence. There is some evidence for a short-lived reoccupation of parts of the South-East; but by 429, when St. Germanus visited Britain on Church business and led the tribal militia to victory over barbarian invaders, there seem to have been no regular troops at all. The great forts of the Saxon Shore stood empty, or inhabited only by refugees, and the patrol galleys rotted in the mud.

Now was the chance for the English to convert raiding into settlement, but they do not seem to have been quick in taking it. It was one thing to leave their homes and families safe behind them and go on a plundering foray from which they could withdraw when resistance gathered: it was quite another to set up new homes in the midst of a hostile and much more numerous British population. The departure of regular troops had not, as is sometimes thought, left the Britons unwilling or unable to fight. Nor could the English bring over at one time sufficient numbers to conquer and hold a considerable part of the island. If the Britons had possessed a powerful central authority, capable of looking to the defence of the

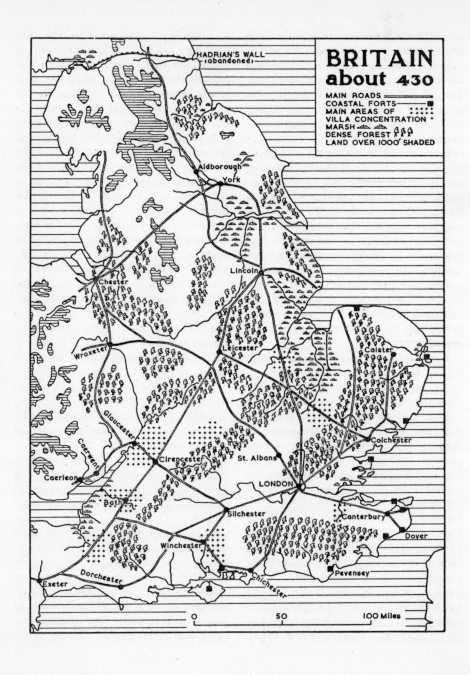

BRITAIN
about 430

MAIN ROADS
COASTAL FORTS
MAIN AREAS OF
VILLA CONCENTRATION
MARSH
DENSE FOREST
LAND OVER 1000' SHADED

HADRIAN'S WALL
(abandoned)

Aldborough
York

Chester

Lincoln

Wroxeter

Leicester

Caister

Gloucester

Caerwent

Cirencester   St. Albans

Colchester

Caerleon

Bath

LONDON

Silchester

Canterbury

Winchester

Dover

Dorchester

Chichester

Pevensey

Exeter

0   50   100 Miles

whole province, it is unlikely that the English could ever have won a foothold.

A central government, however, was just what the Britons lacked. The Roman withdrawal left affairs in the hands of a score of separate tribal units, and these soon ceased to be effective. Instead, power fell to war-lords who were more ready to fight each other than to combine to defend the island, and who were not above employing English war-bands in their own quarrels. It was this disunity, and not personal feebleness, which laid the Britons open to invasion. Given leadership, they were to show that they could on occasion fight as well and as successfully as their Welsh descendants.

Britain in the fifth century was still very much as nature made it. Some forest-clearing and fen-drainage had been carried through in Roman times, but for the most part the valleys remained uninhabited woodland and the low-lying basins marsh. Neglected clearings might take many years to revert to forest, but drainage schemes with their elaborate dykes and ditches would soon go back to swamp. The solid Roman roads, though no longer repaired, still drove straight across these obstacles; but they had been made for troops and officials who no longer existed, or for a peaceful commerce which disunion and disorder had destroyed.

Towns which had once been tribal capitals were now little more than strongholds, whose stout walls might be defended if there were enough people to man them, but whose urban life had been shattered by the breakdown of local government and trade. Villas in many cases had already been ruined, and even the more fortunate and remote were being abandoned because they were no longer safe to live in or could not be repaired. Whatever remained of 'Roman' life in Britain was already fast fading before the English settlements began, and apart from roads and half-ruined buildings the island was much as it had been before the Romans came. But, compared with the large disciplined army and transport fleet of the earlier Roman conquerors, the English resources were pitifully small. Their first great problem was how to establish and hold a bridgehead which should open the way for further shiploads.

THE FIRST SETTLEMENTS

According to the Welshman Gildas, writing about 450, one of the British war-lords was himself responsible for the first English settlement. His story, which there is no reason to doubt, is that about 450 a certain Vortigern, whose power stretched from South Wales to Kent, gave the Isle of Thanet to Hengist and his warriors in return for a promise of armed assistance. For a time they fought his battles, and then, reinforced, turned against him and conquered Kent for themselves. This account rings true. It was a common late-Roman practice to give land to barbarian warrior-bands as *foederati* or allies, in the hope that they would turn their weapons from invasion to repelling new-comers; and much the same thing was done in 912 when the French king settled Vikings in Normandy. Such a settlement was likely to attract kinsmen and new adventurers, and when their numbers were sufficient it would provide an excellent base for further conquest.

9

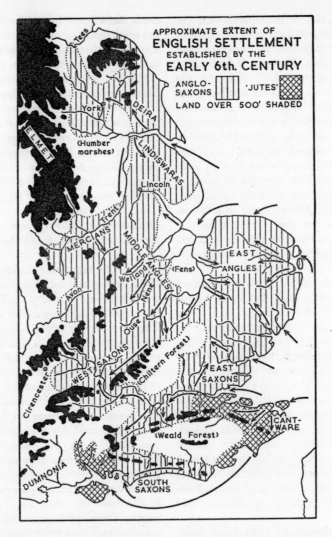

APPROXIMATE EXTENT OF
ENGLISH SETTLEMENT
ESTABLISHED BY THE
EARLY 6th. CENTURY

ANGLO-
SAXONS | | | | 'JUTES'
LAND OVER 500' SHADED

Tees

ELMET

York

DEIRA

(Humber marshes)

LINDISWARAS

Lincoln

Trent

MERCIANS

MIDDLE ANGLES

(Fens)

EAST ANGLES

Welland

Nene

Avon

Ouse

Cirencester

WEST SAXONS

Chiltern Forest

EAST SAXONS

CANT-WARE

(Weald Forest)

DUMNONIA

SOUTH SAXONS

Kent itself then formed for all practical purposes a peninsula which, once conquered, could be easily held. On the west and south-west the great trackless Weald Forest and the Romney Marshes made it secure, and the only open route was between the Thames and the ridge of the North Downs. There are other reasons too for thinking that the English conquest here was more rapid than elsewhere, and that it did not wreck the surviving elements of Romano-British life to the same extent. Here alone, perhaps, did the newcomers take over from the existing lords and land-owners, as they did on the continent, instead of completely effacing the old system to make way for one entirely different. They adopted the British name 'Cantium' (Kent) for the country, and called themselves 'Cantware' (men of Kent). The old centre of the Cantiaci remained the capital as "Cantwarabyrig' (Canterbury) and other sites of Roman towns and forts were used much earlier than elsewhere as local centres. Here, if anywhere, there is a possibility of continuous town life.

The Kentish *ceorl* or yeoman farmer (see p. 24) had an average holding and a *wergild* (see p. 26) twice those of his equivalent elsewhere, and the laws of Ethelbert (c. 600) indicate a large surviving British population. The Kentish farmer also held his land in compact fields, and not in the scattered strips which are typical of other English settlements south of Humber. Whether this was taken over from the Britons or introduced from the Rhineland, it would have caused much less interference with existing agriculture. It seems likely, in fact, that the Cantware were made up of relatively wealthy dominant English and a large number of conquered but not necessarily enslaved Britons. Such a situation might help to explain the remarkable richness of some early Kentish jewellery, drawing on British craftsmen and influenced by contacts with Gaul. Whether the followers of Hengist were really 'Jutes' is, as we have seen, an open question. It is now thought that they also were in origin a mixed band of adventurers, and that the marks which distinguish them from the rest of the English largely developed in Kent from the different nature of their conquest and their closeness to the continent.

There is very early evidence also for Saxons in the Thames Valley. A few graves undoubtedly date from *before* the period of settlement, and may represent members of raiding parties buried by their comrades or possibly 'foederati' living with the Britons. Experts still dispute whether London in the later fifth century remained sufficiently populated and vigorous to defend itself and the surrounding area, but in any case the Surrey heaths and the Chiltern forests were not attractive to settlers. Most early cemeteries are found in the Upper Thames Basin, beyond the Goring Gap, and oddly enough they often lie alongside graveyards of the Romano-British period. This fact would suggest some peaceful contact with the Britons, and some continuity of life in this region. Whether the first settlers came here as invaders or allies we shall probably never know; but from their grave-goods it seems that most of them did not come up the Thames but along the Fenland rivers and across the watershed or along the ancient track of the Icknield Way. The area round the small Roman town of Dorchester-on-Thames (which later housed the first West Saxon bishop) undoubtedly held a considerable English population by the end of the fifth century, and here we probably have the nucleus of the later Kingdom of Wessex.

Another of the earliest settlements, as we should expect, was in Sussex. Here was an area which, in ancient times, was almost cut off from the rest of the country. Between the swamp and inlets of the Portsmouth region, the Weald Forest, and the Pevensey Marshes, lay a narrow tract of habitable downland and coastal plain which was bound to attract settlers once Kent was already occupied. According to the Anglo-Saxon Chronicle, it was in 477 that Aella and his sons with three shiploads landed near Selsey and won a foothold. Thirteen years later they reached and captured the old Roman fort at Pevensey, slaughtering the Britons who tried to defend it. Behind these cryptic entries may lie events somewhat similar to those in Kent: a foothold established by force, confirmed by an uneasy agreement recognising the Saxons as foederati, followed by a building up of strength until the whole area could be overrun. The whole of historic Sussex did not, how-ever, fall within Aella's original kingdom. The settlers of the marsh-bound Hastings peninsula seem to have come from Kent.

Meanwhile, further north, the rivers of the Wash and the Humber were already inviting venturesome boatloads of immi-grants. The Fens themselves were not attractive, and those parts which had been reclaimed in Roman times were already reverting to swamp. The rivers meandering through them, however, gave entry to habitable lands beyond. The light row-boats of the newcomers could travel deep into the interior in search of a suit-able spot for settlement, and the process here was probably much more one of infiltration than of conquest. It was by the rivers, rather than by the barren and waterlogged coasts, that East Anglia, Lincolnshire, and East Yorkshire re-ceived their first settlers. Finally, some-where about 500, the Cantware sent an offshoot past the lands of Aella to colonise the Isle of Wight and the opposite coast and valleys of Hampshire.

The second half of the fifth century, in fact, saw the beginnings of English settlement along the rivers and accessible coasts from Humber to Solent, apparently without any effective opposition from the Britons. If we are to form some idea of what actually happened, we must not think in terms of modern warfare with armies and moving battlefronts. Battles, on a small scale, there doubtless were from time to time, in which lack of unity and organisation on the British side generally gave victory to the small num-bers and determined leadership of the English. Later tradition spoke of Aella as the first *Bretwalda* (see p. 23) and if this means anything it implies that he headed some sort of English fighting confedera-tion in the South-East. But for the most part it was much more a matter of gradual penetration by groups whose object was land, and who were prepared to settle more or less peaceably if they could find it without fighting. The agricultural methods of the English preferred a clay soil, while the Britons in general still clung to the lighter land of the hill slopes. In many parts the English valley settle-ments could exist alongside British villages on the uplands in a state of wary truce.

THE BRITISH RALLY

About the turn of the century this creeping advance received a rude and unexpected check. The Britons found a leader who, according to Gildas, was one of the few survivors of the Romanised ruling class. This Ambrosius Aurelianus organised a stand against the invaders,

Battle between Saxons and Britons, 6th century

and the war-leader Artorius ('King Arthur' of the mediaeval legend) carried on his work. For something like forty years the Britons held their own; and it was probably at this time that the great earthwork of Wansdyke was erected to mark the boundary of a British kingdom of the South-West still holding the chalk uplands of Wiltshire against the Thames Valley English. Behind the later stories of Arthur's 'knights' may lie the folk-memory of a mailed cavalry force of late-Roman type, which would have been very formidable to Saxons who always fought on foot.

We may perhaps see a remote parallel in Alfred's rallying of English resistance when half the country had already submitted more or less tamely to the Danes. Could this new-found unity of purpose have been maintained, the Britons might well have used their still much superior numbers to reconquer the English districts and remain the dominant island race—as Alfred's successors recovered the Danelaw. But it was too good to last. The curse of disunity again hamstrung British effort, and in Gildas' time there were at least five separate British kingdoms in the remaining part of England, besides those in Wales.

The English too were beginning to group into similar units in those parts of the conquered territory which were well-defined by uninhabitable areas of wood, heath, and swamp. Kent and Sussex we have already noted, and Essex between marsh and forest already had some widespread, if sparse, settlement. West of it lay a region which may have formed at

13

APPROXIMATE EXTENT OF THE
ENGLISH
KINGDOMS
C.600
SHOWN UNSHADED: THOSE
SOUTH OF HUMBER ACKNOW-
LEDGED THE OVERLORDSHIP OF
ETHELBERT OF KENT.
Land over 1000' shown in black.

this time one separate unit—Middlesex, between Thames and Chilterns, with Surrey stretching to the Weald Forest. Surrey means 'southern region', and the name implies that it once had connections north of Thames. East Anglia was likewise bounded by fens and forest, and its one good open route to the interior—the track of the Icknield Way—is crossed by a number of boundary dykes which represent early attempts to fix a frontier in the only place where nature had not already done so. Lincolnshire, then called Lindsey (as part of it still is), had similar natural borders: the swamps which then filled the Trent and Witham valleys, and the wooded belt of Sherwood and Hatfield. This area formed a separate kingdom for some time afterwards, and it may be significant that here, as in Kent, the settlers adopted the Roman 'Lindum Colonia' for Lincoln, called the area

'Lindsey', and themselves 'Lindiswaras'. Scarcity of early English finds near the city itself, and the remarkable survival of its double-barrelled name, have led to the suggestion that the British may have held the town until it and they were eventually absorbed into the new kingdom.

Such well-protected coastal areas were doubtless untouched by the activities of Arthur, but the more outlying pioneer settlements in the Midlands and eastern Yorkshire may have been forced into temporary withdrawal. All we can so far say is that Wansdyke is a sign of continued Saxon domination of the Upper Thames, and that the nucleus of Middle Angles and Mercians in the upper valleys of the Wash rivers and the Trent seem to have maintained themselves. In the Vale of York we hear of an unsuccessful British attack on Catterick, which means that the settlements here and on the Yorkshire Wolds (from which grew the kingdom of Deira) were able to hold their own.

THE ADVANCE RESUMED

By the middle of the sixth century the temporary British revival was over, and the English again took the initiative. With the kingdoms of the South-East hemmed within natural barriers, further advance must be made by the inland groups who bordered the British kingdoms and had no serious obstacles to contend with. As yet, however, such groups were too small to do much by themselves: any big advance required larger units as well as effective leadership.

One of the first signs of renewed English expansion was the movement from Yorkshire of Northumbrians, by sea, to the Tyne Valley and the shores around Bamborough about 547. Here at first the followers of Ida could do no more than establish a coastal foothold, and British resistance was strong enough for another thirty years to hold back the development of the new kingdom of Bernicia. It was not till about 580 that conquest began on any considerable scale, and then it took the form of English rule over a large surviving British population.

Meanwhile, far in the South, some obscure movement took place which eventually gave the West Saxons the kings who led them in their dramatic advance late in the century. According to the tradition preserved in the Chronicle, the 'West Saxons came in 514', and landed somewhere near the Hampshire Avon. A series of entries covering forty years tells of the fights of Cerdic and his son Cynric with the Britons of Hampshire and Wiltshire, and as late as 552 we hear of a battle at Old Sarum. This seems in fact to describe the advance of a warband, which gradually fought its way northwards through Hants and Wilts, and eventually made contact with the English of the Upper Thames Valley (where we have reason to believe the 'West Saxons' were already established). These seem to have accepted its leaders, who traced their descent from Woden, as kings: hence the statement that in 560 'Ceawlin undertook the government of the West Saxons'.

From this point we can trace the building of a powerful West Saxon confederacy, soon capable of pushing the Britons drastically backwards. In 571 fighting is recorded at Bedford with the Britons still ensconced in the Chilterns, followed by the taking of Limbury (near Luton), Aylesbury, Bensington, and Eynsham. Since the last two places, at least, were certainly English by this time, this may only mean that more Saxons accepted Ceawlin because of his prestige as a successful war-leader. Not long afterwards, in 577, Ceawlin turned his new strength westwards and, at Dyrham near Bath, defeated the Britons so thoroughly that the Cotswold area, with Gloucester, Bath, and Cirencester, fell finally into English hands. This was a stroke of vital importance, since it severed the Britons of the South-West from their Welsh compatriots and carried the English border to the lower Severn. The West Saxons still had fighting to do in the Midlands, but the Britons were now in retreat.

Further north, in what was to become Mercia, the advance was at first less spectacular, being a migration of groups pioneering in the forests rather than an organised onslaught. Early settlers were crossing the watershed from the Trent into the valley of the Warwickshire Avon, and others pushing along the Upper Trent and its tributaries and into the Derbyshire Dales. In the Pennines, however, the British kingdom of Elmet, behind the swamps of the lower Trent and Humber, defended its hills till well into the seventh century.

ENGLAND ABOUT 600

By 600, nearly two centuries after the last Roman troops had vanished, the English had still conquered little more than half of what was to be England. This area, however, included nearly all the lowlands which had been the most civilised part of Roman Britain, and at this point it would be well to try to reconstruct something of the changes which these two centuries had wrought. Almost every Roman town of importance was now in English hands. Though some, like Silchester and Verulam, had been finally deserted, and at least one—Caistor by Norwich—violently destroyed, most undoubtedly had some sort of life within their dilapidated walls at the beginning of the seventh century. Whether they were 'towns' in any real sense is, however, a different matter, for town life requires a settled and organised society, with established government and trade, and such was hardly to be found outside Kent in 600 A.D. Even such an outstanding place as London is not mentioned in the Chronicle between 457 and 604, and its history between these dates is a blank. There is not a single record of the siege and capture of a town—apart from Pevensey, which was no town but a fort—and the mention of the Cotswold towns in 571 may refer to no more than their ruins and the districts in which they stood. When order and commerce break down, men must live as best they can from the land: and the stoutest walls are no defence to a shrunken and miserable population incapable of manning them. If any were continuously inhabited throughout this period, it can only have been by squatters who eked out squalid existences amidst the ruins of former splendour.

To the first English settlers, a town was an object of distrust to be avoided; a 'tomb surrounded by nets'. Outlaws—and ghosts—might lurk in its silent shattered streets; and if the venturesome chose to satisfy their curiosity by gazing uncomprehendingly on the ruins of bath-house

Early English settlers in the ruins of a Roman town

and forum, they did so by daylight with their spears handy. By 600 some, and certainly London and the Kentish towns, were reviving as life gradually returned to more settled conditions and the advantage of their central sites became apparent. But the timber huts and halls of the English, rising amidst ruined pillars and porticoes, had something of the effect of a Bedouin encampment in the ruins of a Roman city in North Africa. Apart from the site, and the solid town walls, the break in continuity was complete. Even the Roman streets mostly disappeared, though the gates still compelled entry at the same places. This need not imply a long period of desertion, since new dwellings would be easier to build on the old roadways rather than on ground encumbered with ruins: but it does mean the absence of any authority capable of keeping them clear.

As for the villas, they vanished completely. Their ruined buildings were of no interest to the English, and finds of the early Saxon period are almost unknown in them. With the disappearance of town and villa life went whatever remained of the Romanised upper class of Britain. The Celtic-speaking British peasantry, however, remained very much in evidence. In Kent, as we have seen, they may still have formed the bulk of the population, as they certainly did north of Tees. Elsewhere in the conquered areas they were fewer but still widespread, either as refugees in areas unattractive to the English, as villagers still clinging warily to upland farms where the English were not yet established in force, or absorbed among the newcomers as tribute-payers or slaves. It is impossible to estimate accurately how their numbers compared with those of the English, for both Britons and Saxons were already a mixture and nothing can safely be gathered by measuring skulls taken from their graves. On the assumption that Britons were dark-haired and English fair, efforts have been made to provide an answer by

17

TIME-CHART OF THE SAXON AGE

A.D.

Period	Kings	Events
450 — RAIDING		Hengist in Kent. First phase of settlement.
500 — CONQUEST	Aella (S) 477-517 / Cerdic (W) 495-530	British Rally.
550 — AND SETTLEMENT	Ceawlin (W) 560-616 / Ethelbert (K) 560-616	547: Ida founds Bernicia. English expansion resumed. 577: ✗ Dyrham.
600 — NORTHUMBRIAN SUPREMACY	Ethelfrith (N) 593-617 / Edwin (N) 616-33 / Penda (M) 626-25 / Oswy (N) 642-70	597: Augustine's Mission. Union and Expansion of Northumbria. 634: Aidan's Mission. Consolidation of Mercia. 663: Synod of Whitby.
650 / 700	Egfrith (N) 670-85 / Ine (W) 689-726	685: ✗ Nechtansmere. S.W. Expansion of Wessex. Bede.
750 — MERCIAN SUPREMACY	Ethelbald (M) 716-57	
800	Offa (M) 757-96	Offa's Dyke. Viking raids begin.
— RAIDING	Egbert (W) 802-39	
850 — WESSEX SUPREMACY	Ethelwulf (W) 839-58	825: ✗ Ellendun. Consolidation of Wessex.
INVASION / DANELAW	Alfred (W) 871-99	Conquest of Danelaw. 878: ✗ Eddington
900	Edward (W) 899-924 / Athelstan 924-39 / Edmund 939-46	910- Reconquest of Danelaw. 954
Danelaw Reconquered / **950** UNITED ENGLAND	Edgar 959-75	Dunstan's Church reform.
1000 — Second Danish CONQUEST	Ethelred 978-1016	991: ✗ Maldon. Feudal developments.
DANISH KINGS	Cnut 1017-35	Growth of Earls' power.
1050 — NORMAN CONQUEST	Edward 1042-66	1052: Godwine defies King. 1066: ✗ Hastings.

CONVERSION: Church Organised

mapping the hair-colouring of modern Englishmen: but this begs too many questions to be a safe guide. As for place-names, we have the remarkable fact that very few Celtic village-names are found even in Devon and towards the Welsh Marches, where we know survival must have been large. Equally, the names of rivers and hills are mostly Celtic right across the country to the areas of densest English settlement in the East and South. Natural features remain, and the English learnt their names from the Britons: but settlement changes, with different farming methods and variations in rainfall, and many of the British villages on the uplands were in time abandoned for richer soils cleared from the forests. Others were doubtless renamed by new Saxon owners, as English villages later were by conquering Danes. Even where a British settlement remained intact, the name that has come down to us is often not the Celtic one but that which the English used —'Walton' or 'Waltham', the 'place of the Welsh'.

Since in many districts the English must have lived alongside the Britons, it is natural to ask what they learned from them and how the contact changed their ideas and methods. The answer appears to be that the change was nearly all the other way. The peasantry of Roman Britain had known little of Roman life, and for the most part were still untouched by Christianity at the time of the invasions. The civilised upper class had gone under in the turmoil; and though Christianity thrived and spread in the still independent Celtic lands, its adherents showed no anxiety whatever to save the souls of Saxons. Defeated and demoralised, and reduced to dependence or slavery, the Britons of the conquered area instead conformed to the ways of the conqueror. Before long they even gave up their own language for English, and the completeness of this change is shown by the fact that hardly any Celtic words appear in our vocabulary.

When the country again emerges into the light of written history at the beginning of the seventh century, everything Roman except the relics of builders' work has vanished without trace. It is again a land of iron-age peasantry, divided about equally between Celtic and Saxon control, and with as many small and loosely organised separate 'kingdoms' as there had been tribal units in Roman Britain.

THE RISE OF NORTHUMBRIA

The first of the English kingdoms to rise to more than local importance was Northumbria, formed by the union of Bernicia and Deira under Ethelfrith about 605. It was not a final union: it took place by the forcible expulsion of the successor to Deira, and the history of the country down to Viking times was repeatedly troubled by the rivalry of two royal lines both equally tracing their descent from Woden. But in the hands of a vigorous war-leader it made Northumbria for a time the greatest single power in the island. Conditions here were peculiar. Isolated as it was by the great marshes of the Humber basin from Southern England, Northumbria had no such natural frontier with the Britons of Strathclyde, the Picts of the North, and the Scots of Argyll. In the days of its greatness it fought and defeated all three, and for a time controlled Southern

BRITAIN IN 684

THE SMALLER SOUTHERN
KINGDOMS ACKNOWLEDGED
MERCIAN, AND STRATHCLYDE
NORTHUMBRIAN, OVERLORDS.
Land over 1000' in black.

Scotland to the Forth and Clyde as well as North-West England down to the Ribble (or at times the Mersey). The English element in the population was proportionately much smaller than in the South; and its mixture of diverse peoples was one reason for its astonishingly high civilisation in the seventh century, as well as for its chronic lack of unity.

In or soon after 613 we find Ethelfrith defeating an alliance of several Welsh princes at Chester; and by this time the Britons of Strathclyde, like those of Dumnonia, were finally cut off from those in Wales. To Ethelfrith succeeded Edwin, in 616, whose overlordship was recognised by most of the southern kingdoms, and it was apparently he who finally extinguished the British realm of Elmet. He is said to have conquered Man, and to have invaded North Wales. His successes roused against him the odd alliance of the Welsh prince Cadwallon with the pagan Penda of Mercia, which led to his defeat and death in 633; but Northumbria had established too great a lead to be overcome at one blow. Though Penda also defeated and killed the next king, Oswald, in 641, he suffered the same fate himself in turn at the hands of Oswy in 654. The struggle for supremacy continued for another generation, and did not finally tip towards Mercia till Egfrith was killed in 685 in battle against the Picts at Nechtansmere in the far north. Henceforth the power of Northumbria fast declined. Its place as the leading kingdom was taken by Mercia, and most of its conquests at the expense of Britons, Picts, and Scots were lost.

THE BEGINNINGS OF MERCIA AND WESSEX

The 'Mercians' or 'border people' were originally a comparatively small group who settled the upper valley of the Trent and its tributaries. The *march* (borderland) to which their name refers may well have been the forested high ground between the Trent and Severn. They were only one of several separate peoples included in the later Mercia. Earlier, and more numerous, were the Middle Angles who occupied all the district inland of the south-east fringe of the Fens. In the area now represented by the shires of Worcester and Gloucester lived the Hwicce, who seem to have been a mixture of Middle Anglian immigrants and West Saxons who moved in after Ceawlin's conquest of the Cotswolds.

The combination of all these under one leader was necessary before the British could be pushed back from the Severn to the Welsh foothills, and Mercia challenge the Northumbrian supremacy. This apparently was first achieved in 626 by Penda, who claimed descent from the Angle kings in Germany as well as from Woden. In spite of his alliance of convenience with Cadwallon, it was probably he who opened Shropshire and Hereford to English settlement, making room for the 'Magonsaete' and 'Wreocensaete' who appear henceforth among the peoples of Mercia. His son Wulfhere carried his boundaries to the Middle Thames at the expense of the West Saxons, and for a time was supreme in Southern England. Lindsey, too, was finally added to the kingdom after Egfrith of Northumbria was defeated in 678, and for a century and a half Mercia was to be the strongest state in England.

Mercian expansion had the most far-reaching effects on Wessex. The original West Saxon settlements and conquests north of Thames passed into the hands of its powerful neighbour, in Penda's time and soon afterwards; and its whole centre of gravity shifted south-westwards with new expansion into the lands of the Dumnonian Britons. We know comparatively little of the details, but by the end of the seventh century the border had advanced from Selwood Forest (between Somerset and Wilts) almost to the Cornish Tamar. Battles are recorded near

Bradford on Avon in 652 and Selwood in 658, confirming the mastery of most of Somerset, and another in 682 seems to mark advance to the Quantocks. Of the occupation of Dorset there is no record at all; but since no single pagan burial is known in that county, it was probably about the same time as Somerset. Glastonbury, an important Christian site already in British times, preserved its continuity because its Saxon conquerors were already converts. There is some evidence that Saxons were settled in the valleys round Exeter by the middle of the century, and that nearly all of Devon was in English hands by 700. The Welsh kingdom of Dumnonia (which took its name from a tribe of Roman times and passed it on to the modern Devon) still existed in some form as late as 710, when its king Geraint fought the Saxons, but by then it was probably little more than Cornwall.

In these newly conquered lands, the West Saxons were nobles and pioneering farmers scattered amongst a large surviving British population; and here the Britons long remained a distinct race, recognized in the laws of Ine (689–726) and of Alfred (871–899) by wergilds half of their English equivalents in social rank. If their position as a whole was an inferior one, it is clear from the laws that as individuals they could be considerable landowners and even King's Thegns of consequence about the Court. It was good statesmanship to fit them into Saxon society rather than attempt to enslave them; for their numbers were large, and in future troubles their loyalty was to prove vital to the survival of Wessex—and, oddly enough, to that of

Christian England in the crisis of the Danish wars. In fact, the new lands beyond Selwood became the main strength of the kingdom when the old ones were lost or exposed to attack from the north.

The origins of the south-western shires are to be seen at this period, in the settler-groups who took their name from their chief centre. Somerset recalls the 'Sumorsaete' named after Somerton, and Dorset the 'Dornsaete' of Durnovaria or Dorchester.

The growth of Mercia and Wessex had its inevitable effect on the earlier little kingdoms of the South-East. Unable to compete in power, they were bound to be drawn into the orbit of their greater neighbours. By conquest, or tributary alliance, we find them repeatedly subject to whichever of the two was for the time being supreme; and the tendency was for England to be effectively divided into three rather than seven or more units, by the lines of the Humber and the Thames.

KINGSHIP AND GOVERNMENT

By the seventh century, English society had settled down; and with the appearance of written laws and records we can see something of its form. It is clear that the king was of outstanding importance, and that the welfare of the kingdom depended on what sort of man he was. The Anglo-Saxons had never been equalitarians. From the first they recognised an aristocracy of birth, and families with an hereditary claim to rule, and their society was founded on the principle of leadership. At the same time, the king's personal abilities were of such consequence that there could be no automatic succession from father to son. Royal birth was the essential qualification, and it was the business of the great men of the kingdom to choose the most suitable successor from the members of the ruling house. It was quite normal for the brother of the late king to take over (as Alfred did) if his sons were too young or otherwise unsuitable. First and foremost the king was the war-leader; but he must also have a care for the everyday business of government which kept order, dispensed justice, and collected revenue. For these purposes he needed the loyal support of his '*Witan*' or council and his representatives in the shires—the ealdormen. Attempts to read into Anglo-Saxon kingship some form of parliamentary or democratic constitution are wide of the mark. The early English were not given to theorising on such matters, and a king both forceful and popular could act much as he thought fit within the limits of accepted custom. The real check on his power was no set of rules but the fact that in the last resort he must rely on the co-operation of at least the aristocracy. The Witan was no 'national assembly'; it had much more resemblance to the Council of Barons of Norman times, though its membership was never defined. At first it was probably no more than the thegns of the royal household, strengthened in Christian times with the bishops and the king's chaplains. Ealdormen, when kingdoms grew too large to be administered as a single unit, were also appointed by the king from his near relations or personal following. A 'capital' in the modern sense hardly existed. We know of two 'King's Halls', at Rendlesham in East Anglia and at Yeavering in Northumbria, but the king and his court were constantly on the move. They had to be, for the food-rents which farmers paid for their support could not be collected at a single centre. They were delivered at the nearest royal estate, and the court toured round to eat them. Such movement was a fortunate necessity, for it took the king regularly round his kingdom, made him a reality as well as a name to his people, and allowed him to keep an eye on his officials.

From the very first it had been normal for one of the kings south of Humber to be recognised as having some general authority over the rest, whether as a war-leader in the early days of settlement or as a political overlord in later times. The title *Bretwalda* (ruler of Britain) was applied by Bede to a succession of kings ranging back to Aella of Sussex in the fifth century, though it is highly unlikely that Aella himself knew or used the term. By the seventh century, with the appearance of larger kingdoms and more settled boundaries, it implied a position of superiority and power, enforced by conquest or accepted by the weaker kings in the form of tributary alliance. The Bretwalda sometimes treated the other kings almost like his own ealdormen, expecting their support in war, their tribute, and their personal allegiance. It was even thought wise to get his confirmation for grants of land which they made in their own territory. In this way some vague idea of English unity began to emerge, though separate royal houses continued to exist and overlordship shifted with changes of power.

EORL AND CEORL

Next to the king came the *thegns*, the well-born or *eorls*, landowners and warriors with their own estates and households of retainers. Some of them, known as 'King's Thegns', attended the king personally for part of the year; and all were the big men of their own districts, who mustered and led their smaller neighbours in war. In origin they were probably the *gesiths* or bodyguard of the war-leaders of conquest times, rewarded in due course with grants of land. In them we see one of the binding ties of Saxon society, the loyalty to a lord which cut across even the bonds of kinship. It was a point of honour for retainers to devote themselves wholeheartedly to their lord's interests and protection, to give their lives if necessary, and not to return from a fight in which he was slain. This 'heroic ideal' provided a moral code for the warrior, akin to that of the Vikings. It appears in the early Beowulf poem describing events in Frisia before the migration, and it lasts right through Saxon times to the hopeless fights-to-the-death of Earl Brihtnoth's men at Maldon (991) and Harold's housecarles at Hastings. There were, of course, exceptions: two kings in the eighth century were murdered by their thegns. But such cases were so rare as to excite extreme horror. Far more numerous are instances of lives sacrificed to protect the lord in battle or against the assassin, and of death or exile voluntarily shared.

While kings and thegns provided leadership, the main strength of a kingdom (at least in the early days) lay in its *ceorls* or solid yeomen farmers with enough land to support a household. These were the taxpayers, and the bulk of the fighting force in emergency. If they prospered sufficiently to own an estate

comparable to that of a thegn, they might themselves be admitted to thegn-hood. In Kent, as we have seen, they were particularly flourishing and independent, with estates and wergilds twice as large as the normal elsewhere. In the legal sense they were and remained free men, but as time went on their individual importance in relation to the noble class tended to shrink. As kingdoms grew, the king and aristocracy became proportionately richer, more powerful, and more remote, while the ceorl's holding remained much the same as before. It became impossible to gather, or to feed on campaign, the whole force of an area the size of Mercia or Wessex, and fighting became increasingly the business of thegns and their personal retainers alone. Likewise, the grant of royal rights of taxation to thegns, or after the Conversion to the Church, widened the gap. It is one thing to pay taxes direct to the king, and quite another to pay them to a subject.

Below the ceorls came other classes, the half-free and unfree. In Kent we hear of *laets*, who were probably Britons in a state of serfdom similar to that of the villein or cottar of Norman times, and there were doubtless many others in a similar position in other areas of considerable British survival. But sheer slavery also existed. Some of the unfree were of British descent, since the word 'Welsh' is sometimes used as an equivalent for slave; but there were several ways in which English also could be reduced to this condition. Apart from unfree birth, slavery was the fate of unransomed war captives, of criminals who could not find the money penalities and compensations for their misdeeds, and of children sold

24

(in a fashion common till recently in China) because their parents could not support them. Disaster by war, or plague, or famine, was an ever-present threat to the villager with no reserves, and on occasion some were driven by desperation to put themselves in the hands of whoever would feed and protect them. In the eyes of the law the slave (but not the serf or half-free) was part of the farm stock and entirely at his owner's mercy. How he was in fact treated depended on the humanity of his master.

Whatever conditions may have been in the confusion of the original conquest, it is clear that by the seventh century English society was decidedly not democratic, and as time went on its class-divisions widened. As the fighting force came to depend increasingly on the thegns and their retainers, a king who could carry his nobles with him need not be overmuch concerned about the feelings of the rest. In such times this is to be expected; the point would hardly be worth making, had not some nineteenth century historians imagined the Saxon kingdoms almost as crowned republics, with the assembled freemen settling affairs at Folkmoots in the manner of a Greek city state. Such meetings of the shire and smaller units certainly took place, but they met under the king's representative and did the king's business —publication of laws and orders, apportionment of tax burdens, and administration of justice (the profits of which went to the king and his officers).

REVENUE

The support of the king and his household, and of the public business of the realm in war and peace, was provided for by a variety of dues and duties. Besides the produce of the royal estates, to be found all over the country, the king could draw on the food-rent or *feorm*, already mentioned, which all land not specially freed by royal grant paid over to his reeves. This generally took the form of provisions which would keep for some time, such as dairy produce, livestock, corn, honey, and ale. Cash came from fines collected by the courts, tolls paid by merchants, and perhaps from the tribute of under-kings. The property of foreigners who died in the country also fell to the Crown, and various places or estates made special payments for such things as the king's hawks or hunting dogs.

But money, especially in early times, was much less important than direct services. All freemen owed the duty of armed service in the *fyrd*, and the building and repair of *burhs* and bridges. We hear little of burhs before the Danish Wars, but great boundary works like Offa's Dyke doubtless came under this heading. In addition there was the obligation to feed and shelter messengers and travellers riding on the king's business, and to carry timber and other materials for his service. Policework was also, as we shall see, the personal duty of the citizen. Whether any general money taxes were raised in early times is doubtful. They became common enough, as Danegeld, with the appearance of the Vikings, and may have been levied by under-kings for the Bretwalda's tribute. When they do occur, they are based on a land unit called the *hide*—an area originally reckoned to support a household, which varied in different districts

25

from 40 to 120 acres. In Kent the unit was the *sulung*—about double the size.

THE FYRD

To the Saxons some things were so well-known and taken for granted that they never bothered to define them. This is the case with fyrd duty: we hear nothing of the numbers the king could call out, or for how long, or what arms they must provide. Almost certainly every free man was liable, but rarely if ever can they all have been called on. The mustering, movement, and supply of great masses of men was beyond the resources of the primitive kingdoms, and the summer campaigning season was also the busiest time on the farms. As ability to cope with these problems improved, so did the business of war become more specialised. A smaller force, highly trained, expensively equipped, and mounted for movement (though not for battle) would be far more effective and less difficult to manage. Probably for expeditions outside the kingdom the fyrd consisted only of thegns and their retainers, while for repelling an invasion a proportion only of the freemen were called out. The simple spear and shield of the ordinary ceorl were not enough to meet the longsword and axe of the mailed thegn. By Edward the Confessor's time (as we learn from Domesday Book) the usual practice was to send one man from five hides, the rest contributing to his equipment.

LAW AND ORDER

The English brought with them from Germany an elaborate system of criminal law, which was based on the principle of compensation for injury. Detailed tariffs surviving from the time when these codes were put into writing show us that every free man according to his status in society had his allotted *wergild* or man-price, payable to his kin if he were murdered, and proportionate amounts for serious injury, for house-breaking, and for the theft of his property. The normal wergild for the noble class was 6,000 silver pence: for a ceorl 2,000 in Kent, 1,000 in Wessex, and 800 in Mercia and Northumbria. People of British descent, where specially mentioned, were reckoned at half-price. Slaves, however, had no wergild. If their owner killed them he only destroyed his own property, and if anyone else did so he paid their value—usually fixed at one silver pound.

Some crimes were considered 'botless' —beyond money compensation. Such were treachery to a lord, and particularly to the king, witchcraft, poisoning, murder or robbery committed in public, and setting fire to houses—which might cause the destruction of a whole thatch-and-timber town or village. For these death by hanging, and loss of all property, were the answer. In a primitive 'frontier' society cattle-lifting was one of the commonest troubles, and repeated efforts were made by kings to have all sales made before witnesses.

Criminals, then as now, usually preferred to work unseen; and without any regular police-force or scientific methods of detection it was not easy to catch them if they fled, or to prove their guilt if caught. Police methods were those revived in similar conditions in the nineteenth century 'Wild West' of America— the calling out of all freemen to form a

Ordeal by cold water

'posse' for tracking and pursuit. This long survived as the 'hue and cry'. It was not hard to hide and avoid capture in the forests which surrounded the settlements, but anyone who did so condemned himself to a hunted and miserable bandit existence: he was *outlawed*, to be killed on sight.

Trial procedure, with its combination of careful formality and apparent uncertainty of result, is one of the most interesting aspects of Saxon law. In the absence of direct proof, it took the form of an appeal to public opinion, or to the 'judgement of heaven' through the Ordeal. Though of pagan origin, by the time we have any details it had been taken over by the Church and put into a Christian setting. The process was as follows: the accuser formally summoned the accused to appear, and if he refused he was naturally held guilty; if he or his kin did not then pay the due fines and compensations, he was outlawed. If he did appear, the accuser opened by swearing that he was acting in good faith; and the defendant, unless he were a well-known bad character or the circumstances were particularly suspicious, then had to make a count r-oath, backed up by a number of oath-helpers varying with the seriousness of the charge. In a set form he swore— "By the Lord, I am not guilty of act or part in the crime with which I am charged", and his helpers—"By the Lord, the defendant's oath is true and not false". If all this went through without a verbal hitch, he was cleared: but the slightest error would make it void. Oath-helping was a recognised duty of the kindred, but some laws compelled a ceorl to produce at least one helper of thegn status.

If there were witnesses, however, or if the accused were thought too dubious to take the oath, the accuser might bring his oath-helpers instead. Witnesses swore— "In the name of Almighty God, as I stand here freely and unbought, I saw with my eyes and heard with my ears that of which I speak". If the accuser's oath succeeded, or the defendant's failed, the next step was the Ordeal. After fasting, the defendant took the Sacrament, being urged first to confess if he were guilty. Then supernatural judgement was invoked in one of three ways: by cold water, in which the accused, after drinking holy water, was thrown bound into a stream or pond and judged guilty if he floated; by carrying a pound weight of red-hot iron for a fixed distance; or by plunging the hand into boiling water to pick out a stone. For more serious charges the iron weighed three pounds, or the arm was plunged to the elbow. In both ordeals by heat the injured part was bound up, with prayers, and guilt was declared if after three days the wound was found to have festered.

Like witchcraft, the working of this system depended on how far those who took part believed in it. It was not quite as absurd as it sounds, for a man with a guilty conscience would be more likely to ruin his oath through fright, and a doubtful character might find it hard to collect the due number of helpers to perjure themselves on his behalf. There was not then the light-hearted attitude to an oath displayed by so many in the witness box at the present day. It would be rash, too, to assume that knowledge of guilt had no effect on the outcome of the Ordeal, though the state of the bandages may have been equally decisive. The Bedouin to this day use a similar principle, placing a red-hot spoon lightly on the tongue: the guilty and frightened man can produce no saliva, and is burnt.

THE KINDRED

A man depended on his kin for protection under the law, or against the many misfortunes of life. In Germany the 'kindred' was a well-defined group including remote cousins, but in England it is hard to discover just where its limits lay. It was not a clan, for it included the mother's as well as the father's relations, and since marriage was normally outside the group a son's 'kindred' would be different from his father's. In practice we can think of it as the family. If a man were killed, it was his kindred who prosecuted the slayer and collected the wergild —two-thirds to the father's family, and one-third to the mother's. Consequently, if a man had not kinsmen to take action there was little protection for his life. The slayer's kin had the responsibility of finding the blood-money or disowning the slayer: if they did the latter, he became in practice an outlaw.

It was legal, however, to refuse to accept payment and instead to take personal revenge on the killer or his kin; and the *blood feud* thus started might go on with repeated counter-killings for generations. This savage business lasted right through the Saxon period. Alfred tried to limit it to cases where the wergild was not forthcoming, and later kings to the actual slayer, but how far their laws were observed is another matter. Murders within the kindred were beyond the law, for a kindred could not pay wergild to itself or start an internal feud without ending its own existence. If a man had a lord, however, this tie came first. The lord took over responsibility for his misdeeds, while the man could not act against his lord even on behalf of a kinsman wrongfully attacked.

The danger of this system was that a powerful kindred might put itself above the law, by refusing payment, protecting its criminal members, and terrorising its weaker neighbours out of any attempt to get vengeance by force. Readers of 'Lorna Doone' will recognise this situation transplanted to seventeenth century Exmoor. In such a case the only remedy was an appeal to the king or his ealdorman to take forcible action. Cases are known of kings ravaging the lands of people who defied the law, but there must have been many instances of ceorls impotently suffering the oppression of a powerful noble.

Besides its legal obligations, the kindred served many purposes. It arranged marriages, looked after minors and their inheritance, and provided the only form of 'social security' against personal disability or disaster. In Christian times, monks and nuns left their kindred, with other worldly ties, behind them. Their wergilds became payable to their monastery, but if they proved impossible to collect it was left to the king, backed by the spiritual power of the Church, to take vengeance.

Until Christian times there was no way of leaving land and property by will, and it passed automatically according to custom. It seems to have been usual for sons to divide a father's land between them, or for daughters to inherit if there were no sons. The difficulty of this method, still practised in some continental countries, is that it tends to divide farms until the parts are each too small to maintain a household. Possibly in such cases the heirs continued to farm in common. Marriage, as in some peasant countries to this day, was arranged by the parents. It took part in two stages: the 'wedding' or pledging, at which terms were agreed and the bride-price paid over, and the 'gift' or giving-away, accompanied by such feasting as the kindred could afford. Before the Church intervened, divorce was simple; and Kentish laws dating from the end of the pagan period give the wife half the household goods if she took the children. The old Germanic independence of women is still echoed in Saxon law up to the Norman Conquest: they could hold their own land, take their cases to court, and act as oath-helpers on the same terms as men.

FARMS AND HOUSES

Any account of Anglo-Saxon country life must be generalised. Too few dwelling sites have been found and excavated for us to be sure that they were typical, and farming methods were not everywhere the same. We can safely say, however, that outside Kent and East Anglia the two- or three-field system with its open strips, familiar in the Middle Ages, replaced the small enclosed fields of the Britons whereever the soil was not too thin or the land too hilly. This was so even in Dorset, where Saxon conquest came late and British survival was large.

The basis of the English system was the eight-ox plough, capable of dealing with heavy clay soils, together with the axe which patiently and gradually turned woodland into arable and pasture. No-one bothered at the time to describe a plough which was familiar to all, and no remains have been found sufficient to reconstruct it. We know however that it had a coulter for the vertical cut and a share to open the bottom of the furrow; probably also there were wheels to ease its passage and a

mould-board to turn the sod. Oxen, in their slow fashion, have great staying power, and can pull a plough a long way at one draught: but they are awkward beasts to turn. In consequence ploughing was done in long strips or 'furrowlongs', which are the origin of our 'furlong'. Though these were owned separately, ploughing had to be done in co-operation.

Barley seems to have been the most popular crop, perhaps because it also produced ale; but wheat, oats, and rye were also grown where the climate was suitable. Beans and peas appear, but most of our modern vegetables were unknown. There was no fodder crop at all, apart from the meadow hay, and consequently the numbers of stock had to be kept down by a drastic slaughter when the grass ceased growing in the autumn. Woodlands, never far away from the valley villages, provided swine pasture, and cattle made the best of stubbles and rough grazing.

The Saxon village could produce nearly all it needed. Timber for fuel and building was still to be had for the taking, and leather or coarse homespun sufficed for the clothes of the peasant. Two essentials, however, generally had to be bought from pedlars: iron, for spears and implements, and salt for preserving the winter meat. Even if there were a smith on the spot capable of making and mending, the metal itself was found only in limited areas, while salt came from coastal pans or from the saline area in Cheshire.

It was a widely-based economy, but also at times a precarious one. Disaster in the form of cattle-plague, or crop failure, besides war-time ravage, might leave a grim prospect for the following winter, for there was little chance to build

An early English settlement or 'tun'

up a reserve. Diet was at best coarse and monotonous by our standards, and the Saxon addiction to ale and mead may have been partly an attempt to compensate for unpalatable food.

Such evidence as we have about housing illustrates the great differences of wealth and station in early English society. The thegn's hall was a substantial log building, wide and tall, and large enough to be an all-purpose dwelling for the retainers who ate and slept there. Inside the stockade surrounding it were other smaller buildings, the 'bower' for the women's quarters and the sleeping-place of the thegn's family, the barn, byres, and places for the work of the household. Inside the hall were fixed benches along the walls, for seating and for sleeping, and in the middle of one side the 'high seat' of the master of the house.

Long trestle tables were set up in front of the benches for meals, and the space in the centre between the uprights supporting the roof was occupied in winter by a great log fire. Shields and weapons were hung on the walls, partly for display but also because this was the handiest place to keep them, and away from the fire the floor of beaten earth was strewn with straw or rushes.

This was the setting of the evening feasts which were the main 'social life' of Saxon times, with their toasts and saga-telling and boasting. When ale and mead were plentiful, after an energetic day and a good meal, it was time to relax and listen to stories of bygone heroes or brag of one's own prowess and intentions. Modesty was not a Saxon virtue, and boasting was approved so long as it was backed up by deeds.

Early hut of poor settlers, showing timber framework

Royal halls for centuries were only larger and more richly equipped versions of the same thing, though they might have some unusual additions like the 'grandstand' recently found at Yeavering which looks like an open-air council-place or moot. Alfred is the first whom we know to have built in stone. The richer ceorl too might have a 'tun' which was a miniature of the thegn's hall, with its small huts encircled by a hedge.

But the dwellings of the poorest were miserable indeed, unless the sites so far excavated are exceptional. A village of early settlers at Sutton Courtenay in Oxfordshire shows a huddle of small rectangular huts, their floors dug down two feet below ground level to allow their low roofs to rest direct in the earth or on the lowest of mud walls. Another at Car Dyke in Cambridgeshire is much the same. These wretched places were no advance on Neolithic and Bronze Age dwellings of two thousand years before, and life in them was just as squalid. Filth and rubbish were allowed to accumulate on the floors, and bodies were sometimes buried in shallow graves beneath them. Both these villages admittedly date from the earliest days of settlement, and things may have improved later, though this cannot be assumed. Places uncomfortably like them survived in the remoter parts of the British Isles until the appearance of sanitary inspectors.

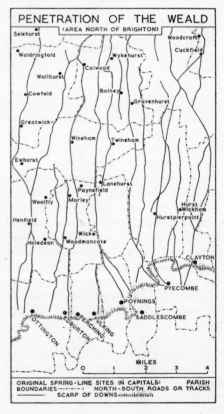

PENETRATION OF THE WEALD
(AREA NORTH OF BRIGHTON)

Selehurst
Woodcroft
Woldringfold
Cuckfield
Wykehurst
Colwood
Wallhurst
Cowfold
Bolney
Gravenhurst
Greatwick
Wineham
Twineham
Ewhurst
Lanehurst
Paynsfield
Hurst
Woolfly
Morley
Wickham
Henfield
Hurstpierpoint
Wick
Holedean
Woodmancote
CLAYTON
PYECOMBE
POYNINGS
SADDLESCOMBE
OTTINGTON
EDBURTON
PERCHING
FULKING

MILES
0   1   2   3   4

ORIGINAL SPRING-LINE SITES IN CAPITALS: PARISH
BOUNDARIES --------   NORTH-SOUTH ROADS OR TRACKS
——— SCARP OF DOWNS ⅏⅏⅏

A Thegn's Hall

Life for the prosperous, whether thegn or ceorl, could be reasonably healthy and comfortable for a people whose standards were not the same as ours. But the wretched hovel-dweller, even if he could feed himself adequately, must have been a prey to all the ills that come with damp and dirt and foul air. Skeletons, as we might expect, show a notable prevalence of troubles such as rheumatism.

PLACE-NAMES

The great majority of our place-names are Anglo-Saxon, and many of them describe the original farming settlement on the site, together with the name of the original owner. 'Ton' (from which our modern 'town') was a 'tun' or enclosure, hence a large farm or village. 'Ham' (whence 'home') meant much the same thing, but on a smaller scale. 'Wick' meant originally a dairy- or stock-farm belonging to a larger place; and others have a similar 'offshoot' significance, e.g. 'ley' and 'den' (clearing or pasture in the forest). 'Barton' means a corn-farm, and 'worth', 'worthy', and 'cot' all imply small isolated ceorl's holdings.

In Sussex the process of penetration and forest-clearing can still be traced on a large-scale map which shows parish boundaries. Along the springline at the foot of the Downs lie the original settlements with names in 'ing' and 'ton', and from them tracks or roads pierce northwards into what was once the Forest of the Weald, reaching the later places whose names include 'ley' (or 'ly'), 'hurst' (wood), 'fold', and 'field'. The parishes, long and narrow, each include a share of downland sheep-pasture, valley clay for cultivation, and former woodland. A similar development may be traced in many areas where the Wessex chalk meets the clay vales.

DRESS

Apart from the early garments preserved in the Slesvig peat, our ideas on Anglo-Saxon dress come mainly from carvings and manuscript illustrations. Only fragments have been recovered from English graves, though these show that linen, and woollens of various types from soft flannels to coarse tweeds, were woven on the upright looms. Fashions varied with the area, and doubtless also with time, but we can form some general picture. There was a great difference between the dress of rich and poor in material, variety, and colour, but the basic pattern was much the same. The prosperous had a linen shirt, trousers belted to the waist and fastened by cross-garters of cloth or leather, and leather shoes. Over this came a tunic, reaching almost to the knees, and a cloak fastened across the shoulders. Sleeved jackets were also worn, and the warrior had his short-sleeved mail coat of riveted interlocking iron rings (or, less expensively, of overlapping rings sewn on to material). War headgear was the conical helmet with an iron frame and panels of iron or hard leather, worn over shock-absorbing padding. The peaceful alternative was the 'Phrygian' cap, like that affected by French revolutionaries.

Dress of the Yeoman Class

Dress of the Noble Class

For women, the dress was a long linen shift, an ankle-length kirtle, a loose-sleeved tunic, and a mantle with a hood. Both sexes loved the bright colours obtained from earth- and vegetable-dyes, and as much jewellery as they could manage. Brooches, pins, belt-buckles, bracelets, rings, and collars of gold or silver, and gold thread embroidery, all helped to display riches, mark social station, and satisfy innocent vanity. Chieftain's graves of the pagan period show that even in the early days there was a surprising amount of portable wealth of this sort for the favoured few.

Further down the social scale cloth becomes coarser, garments simpler and fewer, and ornaments dwindle. A family which spent nearly all its time working on the land (as the huge majority did) must have practical hard-wearing clothes of coarse cloth or leather, though the prosperous ceorl and his wife might well keep something better in hand for festivals. The lowest class made shift with hide and patched rags—as they continued to do right through mediaeval times. It must be remembered that the fine display of the upper class, so often illustrated, was the dress only of a very small proportion.

THE SUTTON HOO BURIAL

England had some fine craftsmen, even in pagan times, to supply the demands of the rich and powerful. Kent has long been famous for its early goldsmith's work, but the recent discovery at Sutton Hoo has proved that it was not so exceptional as used to be thought. This remarkable barrow is probably connected with King Ethelhere of East Anglia, the last pagan ruler of that kingdom, who was killed in

35

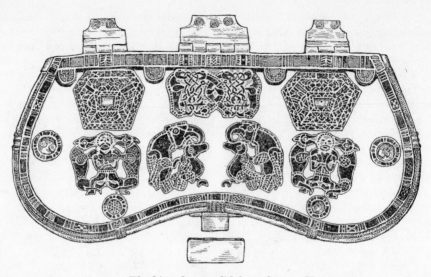

The hinged purse-lid from Sutton Hoo

Yorkshire in 655 when fighting as the ally of Penda. He himself was not buried here: probably his body could not be recovered, but nevertheless a 'cenotaph' or empty tomb was prepared and stocked for him with all due ceremony. Half a mile inland from the estuary of the Deben a trench was dug, and his ship brought over rollers from the water and carefully lowered into the hole. The timber of which it was made has vanished with time, except for a stain in the soil; but the iron nails were found still in position, and with careful digging it was possible to recover the whole shape and plan of the vessel. As we might expect from its date, it was an improvement on the Nydam boat, though by no means comparable with later Viking ships. It was still driven by oars alone, but longer, wider, and deeper in the water. Its hull strakes were still broad, but no longer ran the full length of the ship in one piece: instead, they had riveted overlapping joints. It had been repaired, and had seen much service.

Amidships the 'burial' party had built a special wooden chamber, some 17 feet long, with a gabled roof reaching to the sides of the boat; and inside the collapsed remains of this were found the goods intended for Ethelhere's use in the next world. Swords and spears, an elaborate shield and helmet, a mail coat and clothing, made up his war-gear. There was also a remarkable iron standard, and a curious carved and mounted whetstone which had never been used for sharpening and must have had some ceremonial purpose. But the outstanding finds were undoubtedly those in gold and silver. The goldsmith's work was English, probably made by Ethelhere's own craftsmen, and every bit as fine as, though different from, that of Kent. The purse containing Frankish gold coins has a delicately ornamented lid whose hinges still work as well as when the goldsmith made them; and the mounts and pommel of the sword, the clasps and buckles, are decorated with minute figured inlays of glass and garnets. While the gold indicates the current standards of East Anglian craftsmanship, the silver shows how far-reaching could be the contacts of a powerful seventh-century king. This, by contrast, is all foreign work, and most of it came, surprisingly enough, from the surviving East Roman or Byzantine Empire around the Eastern Mediterranean. How these bowls and spoons reached England we can only guess, but it was probably by way of trade. One large dish had a hall-mark showing that it was already 150 years old when it was buried. Happily, there was no sign of the human or animal sacrifice which often accompanied similar Viking burials.

However hard, and even squalid, the life of the poorer peasant, it is clear that the powerful could command surprising splendour. There is no contradiction in the contrast, for it was by taxing away the surplus produce of the peasants' labour that the king grew wealthy.

TOWNS AND TRADE

The Saxons had several words meaning 'town' which have passed into place-names. 'Burh', now 'bury' or 'borough', meant originally a place fortified with a stockade and perhaps a ditch and a rampart. It could be used, however, of the palisaded homestead of a thegn, or of a strong-point built solely for purposes of war. 'Port', then as now, meant a harbour, but it could likewise mean a market centre far from the coast (e.g. Milborne Port in Somerset). 'Chester', with its dialect variants 'caster' and 'caistor', nearly always implied a Roman site with a wall: it was one of the very few words taken over from the Britons, who had themselves adopted the Roman 'castra' (fort). These words throw light on the origins of Saxon towns. The earliest and often the most important were on revived Roman sites, whose well-chosen position and surviving roads made them again natural centres of population when some sort of town life reappeared. Others grew up gradually as the meeting- and trading-places of newly cleared areas, and some out of burhs whose position proved good for permanent occupation as well as the occasional needs of defence.

We must not read too much into the word 'town' in an Anglo-Saxon context. Most of them differed from villages only in having more inhabitants and in the fact that some of these did not make their living from farming. Many places, and perhaps nearly all, kept surrounding fields under plough, and had their common land and meadow like any village. But as life settled down, government became more organised, and trade developed into something more than packhorse peddling, craftsmen and merchants and officials appeared amongst the farmers.

One very important function of the bigger places was minting. All coins were made by hand, by the primitive method of hammering blank discs between two dies, and as kingdoms grew large this could not conveniently be done in a single place. Moneyers appointed by the king functioned in all larger towns, and struck as much as local needs required. A few gold

Coin of Offa

coins in imitation of Frankish issues were struck in the South-East before 597, and in the seventh century silver pieces called 'Sceattas' became general. Offa introduced the larger and better-made penny about 760, in imitation of the Frankish *denarius* (whence our 'd.' for penny); and this became standard everywhere apart from Northumbria, where base metal *stycas* continued to be struck till the Danish invasions.

Coinage implies trade, and there is no doubt that overseas commerce on a small scale was developing even in the pagan period. The evidence of the Sutton Hoo finds has already been mentioned (page 37); and the discovery of early English coins in Gaul and Scandinavia, and of contemporary Frankish coins in England, shows that the south-eastern kingdoms had links with the continent. Nor were the merchants all foreigners, at least by Offa's time, for his treaty with Charlemagne provides for the protection of English traders in Gaul as well as of Frankish ones in England. Slaves were no doubt a considerable export, and the well-known story of Pope Gregory and his 'angels' indicates that they reached the markets of Rome. So were woollen cloth and hides. But imports were fine fabrics and works of craftsmanship for the

Minting Places of the later Saxon Period. THE MOST IMPORTANT AND PRODUCTIVE ARE NAMED IN CAPITALS.

Coin of Alfred

38

wealthy, which helped to increase the differences between them and the rest of the population.

To cross the seas in search of trade was to face dangers which only large profits could justify. Piracy and shipwreck were normal risks, and anything might happen amongst foreigners. Fortunately, the interest of kings in revenue from tolls moved them to protect alien traders, while being wary to distinguish them from pirates. In 795, when the first Vikings landed on the South Coast at Portland, the king's portreeve rode out from Dorchester in the normal way to see who they were and collect their toll. The Vikings, in their own normal fashion, killed him on the spot.

Men had good reason to be suspicious of strangers, for the line between trade and brigandage was easily crossed and a wandering man might be an outlaw. About the year 700 the laws of Kent and Wessex both provide that a traveller who leaves the highroad must advertise his presence by shouting or blowing a horn, or expect to be slain as a thief. But the genuine merchant, who crossed the seas and cheerfully faced whatever dangers fate might send, was an honoured figure. His occupation had something in common with that of the warrior, and one document suggests that after three such voyages he was entitled to the status of a thegn.

There was a great difference between the first tentative beginnings of trade and town life in the sixth and seventh centuries and the stage to which they had developed by the end of the Saxon period. The Viking invasions themselves proved a stimulus in the long run, for many of the burhs built by either side survived as new towns, and trade with Scandinavia developed on a comparatively massive scale when the period of violence was over. There are even instances of planned towns laid out on new sites, with grid-iron street plans of surprisingly Roman appearance—like Oxford and Wareham—to which settlers were attracted by the offer of privileges and protection. It has been estimated from the evidence of Domesday Book that York had some 8000 people in Edward the Confessor's day, and Lincoln over 6000. At this rate the greater Saxon cities (apart from London, which was much larger) grew to about the size of a small market town of today, and if this is tiny by our standards it was enormous by those of the Saxon village.

The contrast between the English town of the eleventh century and its Roman predecessor of the fourth is instructive. Gone were the grandiose public buildings, the baths, forum, basilica, and amphitheatre: gone too the paved streets and the engineered water-supply. But the Saxon town was at least a natural and living growth, and not the artificial creation of a distant imperial government. It held the seeds of development, while the costly white elephants of Roman Britain had only those of decay.

ANGLO-SAXON PAGANISM

Our knowledge of the pre-Christian religious ideas of the English suffers from the success with which the Church later discouraged mention of the topic. Nor has any pagan temple in England yet been discovered and excavated. We know much about Scandinavian heathenism, which derived from the same source, but we cannot assume that the notions and practices of the sixth century English were the same as those of tenth century Vikings. What little we do know suggests that even the Germanic gods common to both took different forms. In Norse mythology Odin is the father-god, the wise and crafty, with a mass of attributes unknown to the English Woden. The latter appears only as the giver of success in war, or, under his alias Grim, as the maker of great works like Grim's Ditch. Of Thunor, 'the thunderer', we know no more than the name; and Tiw was an ancient Germanic war-god partly eclipsed by Woden. Frig, sometimes regarded as the wife of Woden, was a goddess of fertility. In addition there were Erce, the 'Earth-Mother', and two goddesses Hretha and Eostre of whom we know only that they appeared in the calendar. Of the Norse idea of the struggle between the gods and the giants representing the powers of evil, and of Valhalla where heroes feast after death, there is no trace. There are indeed monsters in the Saxon myths, but they are only man-eating horrors.

There is reason to believe that the worship of these gods was mostly the affair of kings and nobles, and that they did not make much impression on the mass of peasantry. Far more real to ordinary people was the older nature-religion concerned with appeasing by rites and sacrifice the unseen powers which made the crops grow and the stock thrive. So deeply-rooted were these ancient practices, already at least two thousand years old, that even conversion to Christianity did not destroy them. Under a Christian disguise (or

openly without one) the sun-reviving festival of midwinter, the plough-charming of Plough Monday, May celebrations, and the rites of springtime and harvest have survived to the present day.

Animal sacrifice played a great part in both systems, though we find no trace of the human variety which certainly took place in ancient Germany and Scandinavia. Thegn and peasant both, in their different ways, regarded religion as a magical means of ensuring success in this world. Ideas of an after-life there must have been, since they buried property with the dead, but what they were we can only guess. A moral code they had too, but it arose from obligations to a lord or a kindred, or a desire for reputation, rather than directly from religion.

A number of place-names still commemorate sites of pagan worship. Some contain the names of gods, as Tuesley

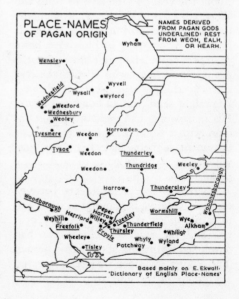

and Tysoe (Tiw): Thundersley and Thursley (Thunor): and Wednesbury, Woodnesborough (Woden). Others derive from *hearh*, a hill-sanctuary, *weoh*, a shrine or idol, and *ealh*, temple. The great majority are in the South-East and Midlands, in parts where Saxon settlement was both early and dense, and none at all have been recognised in East Anglia or north of Humber. Whether this indicates more active pagan religion in the South, or simply the changing of names by later Viking conquerors in the Danelaw, it is impossible to say.

What we know of the pre-Christian calendar we owe to Bede, who was rare among Christian writers in taking a historian's interest in such matters. The year, he tells us, began on December 25th, with the old pagan midwinter festival which the Church adopted as Christmas. The months before and after this were *Yule*, February *Solmonath* (perhaps 'ploughing-month') and March and April named after Hretha and Eostre respectively. It is odd that the great Christian festival should still bear the name of a heathen goddess. May, when the grass grew fast, was *Thrimilci*, because the cows could be milked three times a day. June and July were called *Litha* (perhaps 'sailing-time') and August *Weodmonath*— 'month of weeds'. September was *Halegmonath*—'holy month', when the harvest rituals took place, and October *Wintirfyllith*. Lastly came *Blotmonath*—'blood-month'—when the slaughtering of stock for winter was thriftily combined with sacrifice.

The days of the week still preserve pagan names, but oddly enough they did not get them till Christian times. Our day-names are simply a translation of the Roman ones still used in Latin countries, with Sunday, Monday, and Saturday (for Saturn) taken direct, and Tiw, Woden, Thunor, and Frig inserted as rough equivalents of Mars, Mercury, Jupiter, and Venus.

In the records of early Christian missions we hear of pagan 'high priests', but always in connection with kings. There seems to have been no organised priesthood, and no national centre of worship overriding local boundaries, as in Germany. In place-names, words meaning a heathen shrine are sometimes found combined with names of persons; and it is likely that leading thegns both built temples and acted as priests, as they did in Scandinavia. As far as the official gods were concerned, paganism was not very flourishing in England. It seems never to have recovered from the dislocation of the migrations, and in due course it did not put up much of a fight against Christianity. The ancient folk-beliefs and superstitions of the farming population, however, were a different matter.

Meanwhile, what of the religion of the considerable British population remaining in areas conquered by the pagan English? We know that Christianity was well-established, though not dominant, in Roman Britain of the fourth century, and that before the connection with Rome was broken it was the official religion.* The British Church sent bishops to General Councils, and produced an outstanding heretic in Pelagius. In the fifth century it had sufficient vigour to spread its missionary work over Wales, Ireland, and Southern Scotland. Yet in the con-

*See *Roman Britain*, by R. R. Sellman.

41

quered districts it apparently died without trace, even in Kent where conditions might be thought most favourable to survival.

The reason would seem to be that Christianity in Roman Britain had been largely confined to the Romanised class of town- and villa-dwellers, and had not spread to the peasant mass. Its organisation, as in the rest of the Empire, was based on the cities and their bishops. The English conquest meant the end of towns and villas, and the remnants of the Romanised class either perished with them or moved westwards out of English reach. The depressed and demoralised peasantry who remained had, for the most part, never been Christian. They need not have adopted the worship of Thunor and Woden, for, as we have seen, this was the cult of an aristocracy in which they had at first no share. But in the nature-worship and magical superstitions of the English ceorl they would have recognised much that was like their own ancient folk-practices. The seventh century missionaries noticed no difference between the heathen, whether of English or British origin.

THE CELTIC CHURCH

By the end of the sixth century England (or that part of it in English hands) was a pagan area surrounded on the south, west, and north by Christian peoples. In Gaul the more thoroughly Christianised population, with the cities and their bishops, survived the invasions and rapidly converted their conquerors. Meanwhile, in the Celtic lands a new Church had grown from the fifth century British missions. The Celtic Church, fruit of the efforts of Patrick, Illtud, Columba, and an innumerable host of lesser missionaries, had developed in isolation from Rome. It still calculated the date of Easter according to the ruling of A.D. 455, while the Roman Church worked on a system revised thirty years later. It marked its monks and clergy with a tonsure across the head from ear to ear, while the Romans shaved a round patch on the crown. But far more important differences lay in its organisation and practice. Developing in lands which had no cities, it could not base itself in the Roman manner on the urban bishop ruling the surrounding area as a diocese. Instead, its centre was the monastery: and each monastery was an independent unit, without any defined territory. While the Roman Church was highly organised, with grades of authority culminating in the Pope, the Celts had no central organisation at all. Bishops there were, but only because they were needed to ordain priests: apart from this they had no function or authority, and several are found living together under the rule of an Abbot—or even an Abbess.

Even their monasteries and their idea of monastic life were completely different. In the Roman Church, St. Benedict's 'Rule' (c. 528) had laid down for monks a regular enclosed life, marked by a balance between work and prayer, a sparing but reasonable provision of food and clothing, and complete submission to authority. All slept in common dormitories, ate together in refectories, and remained shut off from the outside world. But the Celtic way was quite otherwise. Not only were there as many Rules as Abbots, but each monk lived separately in his cell, some monasteries included nuns as well,

A Celtic missionary monk

and monks were liable to wander off at any time to look for remote retreats or to preach among the heathen. Asceticism—deliberate deprivation or suffering for the sake of subduing the body—was carried to lengths reminiscent of early Egyptian hermits; and fantastic voyages were made in little skin boats across the seas to places as remote as Iceland. One common practice was to say the midnight Office submerged in freezing water.

Loose as their organisation was, and odd as some of their doings seem, the Celtic clergy had an immense fund of enthusiastic energy and a willingness to take on anything at all for the glory of God. If they were not good organisers, they were first-class missionaries—impressing the powerful with their learning,

the poor with their simple poverty, and both with their saintly example. Heedless of risk or discomfort, they were prepared to meet anyone on his own terms and go wherever the spirit moved them.

A distinction should, however, be made between the Irish Church (and its Scottish offshoot founded by St. Columba) and the Britons of Wales and Cornwall. The Welsh, having passed on the Faith to their fellow Celts, were rather deliberately resting on their oars. They made no effort whatever to convert their Saxon neighbours. With the bitterness of the dispossessed, they took comfort from the thought that though the English had got the best of it in this world, it would be the other way round in the next.

The credit for the original mission to the English must go first to Pope Gregory the Great (590–604), a man of unusual force of character and an outstanding figure amongst the early popes. He rescued Rome from the power of barbarian Lombards and made himself its ruler, did much to spread the Benedictine Rule, and was the first (and for a long time the only) pope to make a serious effort to convert the northern pagans. Legend has it that the idea came to him through seeing fair-haired English children exposed for sale in Rome.

The man he chose to lead the venture was Augustine, the prior of a Benedictine monastery in Rome, and the rest of the party were also Benedictines. They viewed the prospect with some dismay, and only Gregory's insistence stopped them giving up before they crossed the Channel. Yet the position in Kent, their first destination, was unusually favourable. King Ethelbert some ten years previously had married Bertha, the daughter of a Frankish king, and her marriage settlement had given her the right to be accompanied by a bishop and to follow her own religion in Canterbury. Kent, too, had long had close connections by way of trade with Christian Gaul.

Thus, when Augustine landed at Ebbsfleet in Thanet early in 597 he already had friends at Ethelbert's court. This was half the battle, for if he could gain the king's backing it was unlikely that lesser men would stand out against him. The king and his thegns were the mainstay of pagan worship, as well as the accepted leaders of the people, and their conversion would ensure that the mass of men would follow. After some initial suspicion, Ethelbert agreed to be baptised; and Augustine appealed to Gregory for instructions on the organizing of the Church in England. Gregory's answer included much practical wisdom, but showed that he did not properly understand conditions in England. Once the heathen gods were displaced, much of the old system was to be taken over in Christian forms. Temples were to be purified and consecrated as churches, and the old festivals and sacrifices to continue in the shape of Christian feasts with the appropriate merrymaking. "We cannot at once deny everything to such rude natures".

In this way much popular paganism was allowed to continue, under a new guise, with the blessing of the Church, though it is unlikely that many temples proved suitable for congregational worship. But Gregory's ideas on Church organisation proved impracticable. Whether they were based on a memory of the state of affairs in Roman times, or on a knowledge of the important division between Northumbria and the lands south of Humber, they were beyond Augustine's power. Archbishops were to be installed in London and York, each with twelve bishops under them. It seems to have been assumed that the Welsh would co-operate, but when in 603 Augustine met the British bishops near the Severn frontier they refused to accept his authority. They were probably quite as much concerned at the prospect of being ruled by an archbishop based among the detested English as at the idea of submitting to a distant pope.

Gregory died in 604, and when Augustine followed soon afterwards his mission had made little progress outside Kent. Besides Canterbury, bishops had been installed in Rochester and London, and Ethelbert's influence as overlord had persuaded the kings of Essex and East Anglia to be 'converted'. How little conversion of this sort might mean, however, is shown by the action of the East Anglian Raedwald, who played safe by installing a Christian altar alongside the pagan one in his temple. With Ethelbert's death in 616 the hollowness of a conversion which depended on the influence of the great rather than a change of heart was soon apparent. His successor, and the new kings of East Anglia and Essex, were pagans, and their people for the most part followed their example. The Londoners threw out their bishop and did not have another for forty years (by which time Canterbury was too well established as the 'Mother Church' to carry out Gregory's plan of fixing the archbishopric in the later capital). In Kent itself the mission, after its brave start, fell back almost into obscurity. Not till the middle of the century did a reconverted king order the destruction of idols there, and long after this it was still necessary to impose penalties for pagan worship.

Only one further effort was made to carry out Gregory's instructions, when in 627 Paulinus, with his assistant James the Deacon, took the opportunity offered by the marriage of Edwin of Northumbria to a Christian sister of the king of Kent. Like Augustine with Ethelbert, he used this opening to convert the king, with the usual result that the population dutifully presented themselves for a baptism the meaning of which they did not under-stand. Paulinus set up his see at York, and baptised the Northumbrians by troops in the rivers. Given time, and a large band of assistants, this formality might have been the beginning of a real conversion through instruction and preparation: but Paulinus had few helpers and less time. Edwin's defeat by the pagan Penda in 633 appeared as the result of deserting the old gods, and Paulinus' work collapsed like a house of cards. But though he returned to Kent, his assistant James remained with remarkable steadfastness to devote his life to saving something from the wreck.

In 631 a Burgundian monk named Felix arrived in Kent, and was sent on by the archbishop in answer to an invitation from Sigebert of East Anglia. Here he established a mission at Dunwich. But a few years later, in 635, when Birinus came direct from Italy to convert the West Saxons and established himself at Dorchester-on-Thames with the approval of King Cynegils, he seems to have acted quite independently of Canterbury.

THE CELTIC MISSIONS

By this time events were moving in quite a different quarter. While Canterbury for a time relapsed into inertia, the indefatigable Celtic clergy took up the task. Oswald, king of Northumbria, had lived for years in exile at Iona and was already a Christian when he was recalled to the throne. One of his first acts was to invite Celtic missionaries to his kingdom, and though the first arrivals proved faint-hearted the work was taken up in 634 by Aidan of Iona. There was no better man for the job. Able to draw on the king's food-rents for his meagre needs,

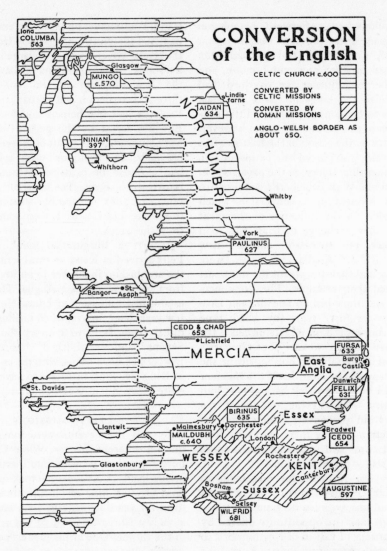

CONVERSION of the English

CELTIC CHURCH c.600

CONVERTED BY CELTIC MISSIONS

CONVERTED BY ROMAN MISSIONS

ANGLO-WELSH BORDER AS ABOUT 650.

Iona
COLUMBA 563

Glasgow

MUNGO c.570

Lindis-farne

AIDAN 634

NINIAN 397

Whithorn

NORTHUMBRIA

Whitby

York

PAULINUS 627

St. Asaph

Bangor

CEDD & CHAD 653

Lichfield

MERCIA

FURSA 633

Burgh Castle

East Anglia

Dunwich

FELIX 631

St. Davids

BIRINUS 635

Essex

Liantwit

Malmesbury

Dorchester

MAILDUBH c.640

London

Bradwell

CEDD 654

WESSEX

Rochester

KENT

Glastonbury

Canterbury

Bosham

Sussex

AUGUSTINE 597

Selsey

WILFRID 681

he tramped the kingdom preaching and teaching, personally meeting people of all ranks on their own terms and in their own tongue, refusing all payment and setting an example of the saintly and self-denying life. His methods were very different from Augustine's, and far more successful. With a growing band of helpers, he laid the foundations of a genuine conversion. Oswald, like Edwin before him, was slaughtered by Penda, but no pagan reaction followed. Under his successor Oswy (642–671) the work went steadily on, and when Aidan died in 651 his monastery at Lindisfarne was providing plenty of monk-missionaries to complete the task.

Northumbria was not large enough for Celtic zeal. Cedd, one of Aidan's disciples, carried the Faith into Mercia before finally settling as bishop in Essex (653–664). His little church in the ruins of the Roman fort at Bradwell still survives, and he founded many others and installed the beginnings of a regular ministry. In neighbouring East Anglia the Irish hermit Fursa had founded a monastery at Burgh Castle in 633, and another, Maildubh, established one at Malmesbury in Birinus' territory about 640. There was even a community of Irish monks at Bosham, amongst the pagan South Saxons. The Celts, in fact, played a part in the conversion of every kingdom outside Kent, and in Northumbria (apart from Paulinus' short-lived mission) the work was theirs alone.

Their very success, however, created difficulties which urgently required solution. About 660 the situation was much confused. In East Anglia and Essex, Roman bishops under the authority of Canterbury found Celtic clergy who owed them no allegiance wandering about their dioceses and, amongst other things, celebrating the Easter feast while they were still keeping the Lenten fast. In Wessex things were even more mixed, since in addition to Celtic activities the Roman bishop there was apparently not under the control of Canterbury. Northumbria and Mercia followed the Celtic way almost exclusively—but King Oswy's queen, and his son who was under-king of Deira, declared allegiance to Rome. Something had to be done, and it was up to Oswy as Bretwalda to do it.

THE SYNOD OF WHITBY

There was far more at stake than the style of clerical haircutting, or even the calculation of Easter. The real question was whether the Northumbrian Church (and in consequence its Celtic offshoots in other kingdoms) should accept the authority of Rome and ally itself with the main body of Christendom, or whether it should remain aloof and thereby allow the existing confusion to continue. There is reason to think that Oswy had made up his mind beforehand, and that the result was already decided before the Synod of leading Northumbrian clergy met in Abbess Hilda's monastery at Whitby.

Cedd was present on the Celtic side and Colman the abbot-bishop of Lindisfarne. But there were also powerful spokesmen for the Roman party—the aged and heroic James the Deacon, who had never left his post since the collapse of Paulinus' mission, and the dour and uncompromising Wilfrid, abbot of Ripon, who had been to Rome and given the pope his personal allegiance. Wilfrid's case was that St. Peter (and through him his successor and representative the Pope) held the keys of heaven, and that to remain cut off from Rome was to risk being turned away from the heavenly gates. Oswy seems to have already had misgivings on this score, and his decision in favour of Rome was probably no surprise to those present. Colman, and others who refused to submit, retired to Ireland. But

47

DIOCESES and leading Monasteries 750

SEATS OF BISHOPS - ■
ARCHBISHOPS - ▦
KNOWN DOUBLE-HOUSES
UNDERLINED. N.B.: THE SEE
OF ABERCORN LAPSED AFTER
685: THAT OF DORCHESTER
MAY HAVE BEFORE 750.
THE SITE OF SIDNACESTER IS
UNCERTAIN.

there could be no question of a general exodus of Celtic clergy: there was no means of replacing them, and they could not be expected suddenly to change their whole mode of life to fit into the Roman pattern. Conformity on the date of Easter, and a general acknowledgement of papal authority, was all that could be immediately expected.

Oswy's decision at Whitby in 663 was not the final solution of all problems, but it was a decisive step in that direction. Other English kingdoms soon came into line, and before very long the Celtic ones

48

also. It was now up to Rome to accept the offered opportunity, and to complete with its powers of organisation the work of erecting an English Church on the foundations prepared by Celtic missionary genius.

THEODORE OF TARSUS

Before anything could be done a plague swept England with disastrous consequences to monks and clergy. Bishoprics fell vacant and were not filled for years, and those priests who performed their duties to the sick most faithfully were the first to die. Not till 668 did the pope appoint a new archbishop, but his choice, if belated, was fortunate. Theodore of Tarsus was already an old man of 66, but he still had twenty years of vigorous life ahead. His friend and helper Hadrian, a North African who had been abbot of a monastery near Naples, was to survive as Abbot of Canterbury for forty years.

On his arrival in 669, Theodore found a lamentable state of affairs. South of Humber there was only one bishop in the country, and he had bought the see of London. In Northumbria there were two —at loggerheads. Wilfrid of York, returning from consecration in Gaul, had found his see usurped by Cedd's brother Chad—who had been consecrated by Welshmen, and was therefore in any case dubious from the Roman point of view. Without bishops to ordain priests and exercise authority there could be no progress, and Theodore's first concern was to install suitable men at Rochester, Dunwich, and Winchester, and to remove Chad, duly reconsecrated, to a new Mercian see at Lichfield. Each kingdom now had its own bishop, but Theodore's object was to make the Church a unity taking no account of political boundaries. To assert the authority of Canterbury, and make churchmen conscious that they were members of one body, he called the first Council of the English Church at Hertford in 672. The first task was to bring the wandering Celtic clergy under the control of the diocesan bishop. Monks were forbidden to leave their monasteries without the abbot's consent, and clergy to move about the country without their bishop's licence. If priests and bishops had to travel into another diocese, they were not to perform their functions as churchmen without the leave of the bishop in whose territory they were.

It was clear to Theodore that a single bishop could not cope with the work of an area the size of Northumbria or Mercia, but when he suggested the division of dioceses into more manageable units the existing bishops protested. Rather than cause unpleasantness and conflict, he wisely bided his time and then divided the sees as they fell vacant. When the Bishop of Dunwich retired he created a separate diocese for the 'North Folk' of East Anglia at Elmham; and when Chad's successor at Lichfield was deposed for disobedience he took the opportunity to create separate bishoprics for the Middle Angles at Leicester, for Lindsey at Lincoln, for the Hwicce at Worcester, and for the new settlers beyond Severn at Hereford. The expulsion of Wilfrid from York by King Egfrith as the result of a long-standing personal quarrel gave the chance to make new sees at Hexham, Lindisfarne, Abercorn, and Ripon. Undaunted, Wilfrid retired to the one surviving heathen area—Sussex and the Isle

49

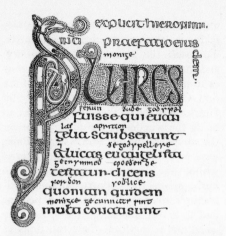

*Part of a Latin manuscript with an illumin-
ated capital and English words interlined*

of Wight—and for the next five years
busied himself with their conversion. The
result of his labours was the South Saxon
diocese based on Selsey.

By Theodore's death in 690 there were
fifteen bishoprics, and a national Church
under one archbishop had replaced the
former division by kingdoms. His successor recognised the recent westward
expansion of Wessex by erecting a further
see at Sherborne in 705 for the new lands
beyond Selwood, and in 735 York was at
last elevated into a second archbishopric,
according to Gregory's original plan. But
Offa's later effort to set up a third archbishop at Lichfield was a step backwards
towards the division on political lines
which Theodore had laboured to end.
The attempt was short-lived, and the first
Mercian archbishop had no successor.

SCHOOLS AND LEARNING

One of the first necessities for an
organised Church was an adequate supply
of properly trained priests, and Augustine's mission set up training schools in
connection with its cathedrals. We know
little about them, however, beyond the
fact that they provided instruction in the
Latin necessary for the use of the service
book and the scriptures, and in chanting
and the Church calendar. Theodore's
foundation at Canterbury was much more
enterprising, including some Greek in its
curriculum, but the chief centres of
seventh century learning were undoubtedly Celtic. One of the glories of the
early Irish Church was the remarkable
standard of scholarship it maintained, in
conditions of poverty and virtual isolation. It was from the Irish, not from
Rome, that the English learned the clear
and beautiful letters used in their manuscripts, and the art of illumination. Not
surprisingly, therefore, Northumbria with
its close Celtic contacts developed much
the richest culture in England during the
century after the Conversion. Apart from
the copying of books, and later the writing of new ones, the Northumbrians
developed the art of the tall stone Cross
with its elaborate carvings, which they
used as memorials or to mark places of
worship before the building of churches.

It is no accident that the first outstanding English literary figure is the
Venerable Bede (c.671–735), born near
Jarrow in County Durham and never
known to have travelled outside Northumbria. At the age of seven his parents
put him in the care of Benedict Biscop—
one of Theodore's pupils—in the monastery of Monkwearmouth, and here, and
later in the daughter house at Jarrow, he
spent all his long life. From a series of
journeys to Rome, Benedict had got to-

gether an outstanding library; and with this to hand Bede could draw on the best continental scholarship of his time without stirring from his monastery. He produced a mass of religious works and scriptural commentaries, but the book by which he is most remembered in his 'Ecclesiastical History of the English Nation'. This remains our chief source for the events of the Conversion period; and its style, and the care which Bede took to gather information from all parts of the country, show that he had a regard for historical fact which was rare in an age when most writers were content with sermons or pious fables.

Stone cross, Irton, Cumberland

From Bede we know of Caedmon, the cowherd of Whitby (another Northumbrian) who is sometimes regarded as the 'father of English poetry'. Much that is attributed to him may be by other and unknown hands, but the purpose of all these works is to present Christian themes and Old Testament stories to a people used to the language of the sagas. God appears as a mighty king attended by thegns, and Satan as a rebel war-leader with his retainers. Battles between the ancient Israelites and their foes are described with a wealth of detail as though they were fights between English and Britons. Later poems attributed to the West Saxon Cynewulf concentrate rather on the New Testament, but even here the Disciples appear in the guise of battleworthy thegns, 'active in the fyrd'. The Beowulf story is a survival from pagan times, edited before writing so as to fit into a Christian setting: but in general the Church preferred that the old tales should be forgotten, and that Christian ones, written in a style the English could appreciate, should take their place.

The newly converted English caught something of the Irish missionary zeal. From the end of the seventh century for a hundred years Englishmen worked to convert the Frisians and Germans, aided by their similarity of language and outlook. The West Saxon Wynfrith (or Boniface), with English helpers and books, founded an organised Church with bishoprics and monasteries in the Rhineland and South Germany.

THE INFLUENCE OF CHRISTIANITY

It would be too much to expect the high standards of selfless sainthood shown by outstanding men in the age of conversion to continue without some relaxation. The century after Bede produced fewer exceptional individuals, but at the same time it was a period of solid if unspectacular work, carrying on the organisation of the Church and making Christianity a reality to the many who had at first accepted it only on the surface. The Christian leaven worked, through its teachings, the law, and the system of penance, to soften some of the crudeness of Saxon life.

From the first, leading churchmen worked in close alliance with kings. While they needed the royal protection, they had much to offer in return. They strengthened the king's position by introducing a ceremonial coronation which made him 'the Lord's anointed', and, though the Witan's right to elect was unchanged, it came in time to be held that a king once consecrated could not be deposed. The Church was of course unknown to Germanic customary law, and to fit it into English society it was necessary to draw up written codes which gave churchmen the protection of wergild and compensation. A way had likewise to be found which would get round the strict law of inheritance and allow the Church to be endowed, and the result was the 'land-book' or title deed by which land could be granted, and the 'will' by which it could be bequeathed.

But the influence of the Church was by no means confined to securing its own interests. Efforts were made to mitigate the barbarity of slavery and the blood-feud. With bishops and the king's chaplains now taking a leading part in the Witan, there was plenty of opportunity to press the Christian point of view. Slavery was not condemned outright: bishops possessed slaves, though a Church Council of 816 ruled that they must be freed on the bishop's death. The Church strove rather to work gradually, giving the slave some rights and some hope of eventual freedom. Later laws laid down that they must have some free time in which to earn on their own account, and the right to keep earnings towards buying their liberty. Provisions were also made for a reasonable standard of maintenance. Besides legal protection, much was done by influence and persuasion to encourage laymen to free their slaves, especially at the master's death; and the spiritual penalties of penance, and if necessary excommunication, were invoked against brutalities which the law did not punish. A man who freed his slave kept the right to collect his wergild if he were killed, so that he was not left without a protector.

By the development of the system of private confession and penance, which Theodore adopted from the Celts, the Church strove to enforce a Christian moral code which went far beyond the letter of the law. Penance on bread and water was prescribed according to the seriousness of the offence and the standing of the offender. Drunkenness, the besetting Saxon vice, was not only bad in itself but also a source of quarrels and violence. Laymen who drank themselves sick were ordered five days penance by Theodore, but monks thirty days and priests or deacons forty. Archbishop Egbert of York went further in dealing with those who drank to unsteadiness: three days for the layman, but two weeks for the monk, four for the priest, and five

Stone Saxon church at Bradford-on-Avon

for the bishop. Lapses of all kinds were catered for—including practices which were not so much immoral as merely filthy, like drinking foul water or eating animals which had died of disease.

The system was excellent in intention, and doubtless also to a large degree in effect, though there are signs that it proved in the long run too severe for still unregenerate humanity. Egbert allowed penance to be worked off by cash or by prayer instead of fasting, and this opened a way for evasion.

THE PARISH SYSTEM

It was some time before Christian teaching, and the Sacraments, could be brought within reach of everyone, and centuries before each village had its priest. In the first period of conversion the only centre was the bishop's household with its band of clergy, or in Celtic areas the monastery-mission. As the number of priests grew, however, it was possible to set up churches served by a body of clergy who operated over a large district of many villages. These, known as 'Minsters', are often still commemorated by modern place-names (though the same word also meant an ordinary monastery). Crosses were often set up to mark spots about the countryside where minster priests preached and conducted services on their rounds.

The founding of village churches was mostly left to local thegns or landowners, who built them, appointed a priest, and allotted some land in the open fields for his maintenance. Such churches remained the founder's property, to sell, bequeath, or even demolish; and since the rough timber buildings have long vanished, and the endowment was generally too small for a written charter, little evidence remains of the beginnings of our parish system. A few examples of churches built in stone survive, generally in places which were too poor in later times to afford rebuilding, but these mostly date from late in the Saxon period. The difference between Roman and Celtic ideas is shown even in church plans. Those connected with the Kentish mission are copies of the continental basilica, with nave, aisles, and apse, but the Celtic style (far more widespread and long-lasting) is a simple rectangle, with the sanctuary at the east end separated by an archway.

Parish priests differed from their parishioners only in their training and their Office. They were drawn from the likelier boys of the ceorl class, and their style of living remained that of the peasant. Apart from occasional fees they had to support themselves by work on the land like any other ceorl, and therefore fully shared the life of their flock. The existence among the villagers of a man who was one of themselves, and yet had some education and some experience of a wider life than that of the village, must have had a civilising influence unknown to heathen society.

Tithe-paying began in the seventh century as a moral, but not yet legal, duty. At first the proceeds were used for the support of the poor as well as the clergy, and only gradually did it become a compulsory payment for the support of the minster or the local church.

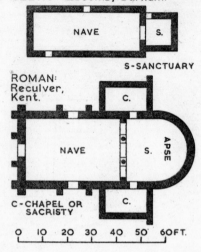

SEVENTH-CENTURY CHURCHES:
CELTIC: Escomb, Durham.

NAVE   S.

S-SANCTUARY

ROMAN:
Reculver,
Kent.

C.

NAVE   S.   APSE

C-CHAPEL OR
   SACRISTY

C.

0   10   20   30   40   50   60 FT.

MONASTERIES

The destruction in the Danish wars of at least half the monasteries in England, with their books and records, and the decay of the rest, has left us short of information on their early history. What we do know, however, suggests that it was extremely diverse. The Benedictine Rule was by no means strictly followed everywhere, even after Theodore's time. At Canterbury itself the cathedral monks are found owning private houses in 813, and shortly before this the Abbot of Worcester bequeathed a private inheritance which, properly speaking, he should not have possessed. Between great royal foundations and small local houses founded and largely run by laymen, often on a family basis, there was a tremendous difference. Bede himself complains of bogus foundations designed as a means of tax-evasion, with lay abbots and retainers masquerading as monks. It is, of course, easy to make too much of statements of this sort, but there was undoubtedly something in them. Monasteries, and especially nunneries, were often used as convenient retreats by people who had no real vocation for the religious life, and who introduced worldly luxuries and amusements which had no place there. In 747 a Church Synod was moved to order that bishops should inspect monasteries annually and make sure that the inmates were observing the Rule and the seven daily services. Bright clothing and drunkenness (both of which the Saxons found it hard to forgo) were to be avoided, and laymen and entertainers kept out.

We need not be surprised if ideal standards of saintliness were not always and everywhere respected. Saints are exceptional at any time, and if there had been enough of them to fill the many houses which appeared in the pre-Viking period the Saxons would indeed have been a remarkable people. If some monasteries were not notable for a pious and regular life, they were at least places of civilised living: and the better ones were citadels of religion, learning, and the Arts. It would be fairer to contrast them, not with the ideal they sometimes failed to reach, but with the illiterate pagan barbarism they so closely followed.

One interesting development was the double-monastery, designed for monks and nuns together under the control of an abbess. These were of course not 'mixed' in the school sense: monks and nuns might join in worship in the same church, but otherwise they lived quite separately. At Wimborne the abbess controlled her monks by giving orders from a window. The abbesses of these foundations were often of noble or royal birth, and noted for their ability and character. The arrangement seems to have been Celtic in origin. The idea of an abbess ruling monks must have seemed odd to people brought up in the continental assumption of male superiority, but it fitted in with Saxon ideas of the dignity and equality of women.

The Conversion brought deep, if gradual, changes in English life. It did not immediately make saints of more than a few exceptional Englishmen, but it did bring a more humane outlook in law and everyday behaviour. By reopening contact with lands which preserved much of their Roman heritage, and with the isolated brilliance of Ireland, it brought England for the first time into the fold of Western civilisation. The result in the long run was that peculiar blend of Germanic qualities and traditions with Roman and Christian influences which forms the background of our national culture. To compare King Alfred, in whom this mixture is personified, with the outstanding figures of pagan times is to see the magnitude of the change.

THE SUPREMACY OF MERCIA

By the time Bede was writing his Ecclesiastical History, the brief Northumbrian supremacy was over and its brilliant culture was in decline. The divisions of this unhappy kingdom, suppressed by the great kings of the seventh century, broke out afresh and reduced it to impotence. The monarchy became the prize of violence, and in the course of a hundred years five kings were murdered or killed

by rebels, five deposed, and four obliged to abdicate. In the north the earlier supremacy over Picts and Britons was lost and the frontier retreated, while southwards the growing power of Mercia overshadowed all England.

The eighth century is the period of Mercian Bretwaldaship, under the two great and long-lived rulers Ethelbald (716–757) and Offa (757–796). The latter was the first to use the title 'King of the English', and his conquests went far towards making it a reality. Essex was already virtually a Mercian province, and the dependent Hwicce were now incorporated. In 771 Offa took the submission of Sussex and conquered the Haestingas.

Shortly afterwards, in 775, he overran Kent, and henceforth ruled it as part of Mercia. East Anglia was annexed in 794, and before his death everything south of Humber was Mercian save Wessex, which he had defeated and deprived of Berkshire in 779. With Wessex and Northumbria he was content to remain on terms of overlordship, making marriage alliances with both. The Welsh he harried repeatedly, till he marked a final boundary with the immense earthwork still called 'Offa's Dyke'. This rampart, running from near Flint on the north coast to the upper Wye, is not continuous, since it was not thought necessary to carry it through stretches of trackless woodland. It must

56

not be thought of as a 'Hadrian's Wall' manned by garrisons: Offa was not thinking in terms of defence, but of marking the frontier in an obvious and indestructible fashion as a warning of the consequences to any Welshman found on the wrong side without a plausible excuse.

Offa's greatness was recognised abroad. He treated on equal terms with Charlemagne; and the Pope, who addressed him as 'Rex Anglorum', permitted him to set up his own archbishopric at Lichfield. Offa in return undertook to make an annual payment to Rome of 365 mancuses (of 30 pence), which was the origin of the mediaeval 'Peter's Pence'. We have already seen that he was the first to adopt the continental penny as the standard coin, and one example survives of a most remarkable issue in gold copied direct from the dinars of the Moorish Caliphs. This would have been worth about thirty silver pennies, and may be the 'mancus' used in the papal payment. If so, His Holiness must have thought the Mercian moneyer's attempt to copy an Arabic inscription from the Koran somewhat inappropriate.

Offa's greatness, however, cannot be compared with that of Alfred. It was founded on superior force ruthlessly used, and Englishmen were not to be united on those terms. When force failed, as it did under his successors, the conquered areas took the first chance to throw off the Mercian yoke. Indirectly he contributed to the later rise of Wessex, for the lesser kingdoms were only too glad to transfer allegiance to anyone who would protect them from Mercian bullying. The men of Kent rebelled as soon as they heard of Offa's death; they were defeated for the moment, but Mercian power shrank rapidly.

THE RISE OF WESSEX

With Mercia following Northumbria into decline, the supremacy passed (finally, as it turned out) to the House of Wessex. Egbert (802–839) was of the Kentish as well as the West Saxon royal line, and as such he had been forced into exile by Offa. For three years he lived at the court of Charlemagne, and it is likely that he learned there much of the craft of kingship and empire-building which he later put to good use as ruler of Wessex. Of his early years as king we hear little, apart from the reduction of Cornwall in 814. For twenty years he seems to have accepted quietly the waning overlordship of Mercia, while preparing to turn the tables. Then in 825 he struck hard, and at one blow the empire of blood built by Offa collapsed. His defeat of Beornwulf of Mercia at Ellendun (near Wroughton, on the edge of the Marlborough Downs) was quickly followed by the willing submission of Kent, Surrey, Sussex, and Essex. Even East Anglia, anxious to pay off old scores, rose and killed Beornwulf and put itself in Egbert's hands. In 829 Mercia itself was conquered, and ruled directly for a year or so until Egbert restored its native ruler as under-king. The Northumbrians acknowledged Egbert's Bretwaldaship, and in 830 he even victoriously invaded North Wales.

His rapid success was no momentary achievement, and its results did not end with his death. The conquest of Cornwall proved permanent, and the Cornish attempt to recover independence with the help of a Viking army in 838 was crushed

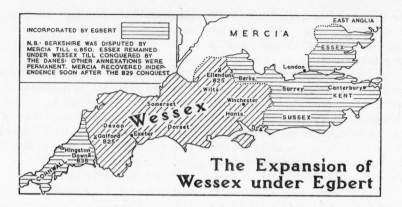

INCORPORATED BY EGBERT

N.B.: BERKSHIRE WAS DISPUTED BY MERCIA TILL c.850. ESSEX REMAINED UNDER WESSEX TILL CONQUERED BY THE DANES: OTHER ANNEXATIONS WERE PERMANENT. MERCIA RECOVERED INDEP- ENDENCE SOON AFTER THE 829 CONQUEST

MERCIA

EAST ANGLIA

ESSEX

London

Ellendun 825

Berks.

Wilts.

Surrey

Canterbury

KENT

Somerset

Winchester

Hants.

SUSSEX

Wessex

Devon

Dorset

Exeter

Galford 825

Hingston Down 838

CORNWALL

The Expansion of Wessex under Egbert

by a further victory at Hingston Down near Plymouth. The south-eastern king-doms too were finally incorporated. They could no longer exist separately, and they threw in their lot willingly with Wessex. The lands north of Thames could not yet be firmly controlled from Winchester, but everything south of it now formed a single compact kingdom, unified by the ridgeways of the chalk hills. The Wessex line continued to produce great kings, and the acid test of the Viking onslaught proved that they could defend their realm when everything else disintegrated. As the only royal line to survive the Danish deluge, they in due course exchanged Egbert's vague Bretwaldaship for the unified rule of a single Kingdom of England.

KING ALFRED

The story of the Viking raids and invasions which led to the conquest of half England (the Danelaw), and a century later to that of the whole country after it had been united by the kings of Wessex, has been told elsewhere.* Nothing better

*See *The Vikings*, by R. R. Sellman.

illustrates the importance of the king in Saxon history than Alfred's successful resistance to the Danes after disasters which would have driven a lesser man to despair and flight. His leadership alone saved Wessex from going the way of all the other kingdoms, and preserved Christian civilisation in England from 'the fury of the Northmen'. To the best heroic traditions of the Saxon race Alfred added love of learning, statesmanship, and a deep religious faith. With these, too, he had qualities remarkable indeed in a Dark Age king—an insatiable curio-sity about the world and the workings of nature, and a concern with the deeper problems of life and death.

It was not enough, for him, to beat Viking aggression to a standstill: the whole fabric of ordered civilisation had been shaken in the conflict, and his aim was to rebuild it better than before. Confidence in law and order must be restored, and to that end he not only amended and re-coded the law but ensured by constant personal supervision that it was respected. The monarchy, and the ealdormen and nobility through whom it ruled, emerged stronger than ever. But Alfred's ideas ranged far beyond the punishment of evil-doers. He aimed to educate his people to an understanding of their religion and their history, and to make them civilised and law-abiding by conscious choice. The task was so enormous, and the means so slender, that no-one but Alfred would ever have attempted it. If the results fell short of his hopes, it remains astonishing that any ruler of the Dark Ages (or for that matter of much later times) should not only have thought on these lines but have made great personal efforts to push the work forward.

Alfred had first to educate himself. Two visits to Rome in early childhood had

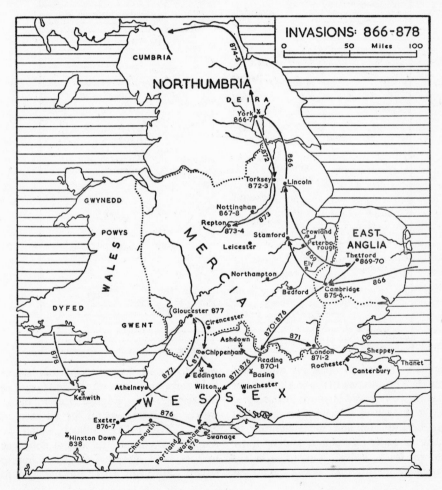

ENGLAND c.910:
APPROXIMATE LIMITS OF THE
DANELAW: - - - -
CENTRES OF SEPARATE JARL-
DOMS NAMED IN CAPITALS.
ENGLISH BURHS (INCLUDING
THOSE BUILT EARLY IN THE
RECONQUEST) UNDERLINED.
0   25 Mls. 50   75

ENGLISH NORTH-UMBRIA

(NORSE SETTLERS FROM IRELAND)

Carlisle

Whitby

Scarborough

KINGDOM OF YORK

York

Grimsby

Manchester

Warburton

Runcorn

Chester   Eddisbury   Bakewell

LINCOLN

DERBY

NOTTINGHAM

DANISH MERCIA

Stafford

Shrewsbury

STAMFORD

Tamworth

LEICESTER

Kgdm. of

Chirbury

Bridgnorth

Warwick

ENGLISH MERCIA

HUNTINGDON

Thetford

EAST ANGLIA

NORTHAMPTON

Worcester

Hereford

Towcester

BEDFORD

CAMBRIDGE

Buckingham

Wing

Colchester

Gloucester

Witham

Cirencester

Oxford

Hertford

Maldon

Cricklade

Wallingford

London

Bath   Malmesbury

Southwark

Rochester

Watchet

Axbridge

Tisbury

Eashing

Canterbury

Pilton

Atheney

Shaftesbury   Wilton

Winchester

Lydford   Exeter

Southampton

W E S S E X

Bury   Lewes

Wareham

Chichester

Hastings

Halwell

Bridport

Twineham

Porchester

doubtless helped to open his mind and stimulate his interest in the world, but the teaching he received in youth was meagre. Yet at the age of forty, with a desperate war behind him and more fighting to come, he gathered teachers and set himself to learn Latin. Famous scholar-priests from Mercia, Wales, and the continent were invited to join his household and assist him with the great work of translating into English those 'books which are most needful for all men to know'. The Palace School which he founded, to educate the sons of nobles as well as boys intended for the Church, taught Latin: but Alfred did not wish to

60

Alfred at work with his priests

keep education as the privilege of the few. Many more could learn at least to read their own language, and he urged the bishops to set up schools for 'all the free youth in England' who could be spared from the plough. It was for these that he and his helpers translated, and had copied and distributed, Pope Gregory's *Pastoral Care* (a book instructing clergy in their duties to their flock), Bede's *Ecclesiastical History*, Orosius' *History of the World up to the fall of Rome*, and other outstanding works of philosophy and religion, as well as the newly compiled *Anglo-Saxon Chronicle*. In the later translations Alfred's own hand increasingly appears, adding facts and ideas. In Orosius he inserted a section on the geography and life of the Baltic lands and Scandinavia, gleaned from seafarers visiting his court.

It is typical of Alfred that all his wars were defensive, or counter-strokes against attack. The only territory he added to his realm was London and the land to the northward, taken from Guthrum after an unprovoked breach of their original treaty. The remaining English half of Mercia he effectively controlled through its ealdorman, yet he never attempted to annex it to Wessex. Even with Danes he was ready to make peace and live amicably as soon as they would do likewise. Yet his influence throughout England was immense. His personal qualities, as well as the fact that he was the only surviving Christian king, made Englishmen throughout the Danelaw regard him as their natural leader, and even the Welsh princes sought his friendship and protection. His successor's task in reconquering the Danish lands and making England one kingdom was thus made much easier by the new willingness of the English outside Wessex to forget old divisions and rivalries and accept its royal House as their own.

Great kings, in the days of personal rule, were seldom good men, and saintly characters seldom made good kings. Power and force of character too often resulted in ruthlessness and aggression, while mildness and concern for spiritual matters were apt to mean weakness and irresolution in affairs of state. It is Alfred's glory that he combined goodness, thoughtfulness, and a deeply personal religion with common-sense, decisiveness, and continual devotion to his duty as king. "It has always been my desire", he wrote, "to live worthily, and after my death to leave a memory of good works to posterity". There is an echo here of the pagan 'heroic ideal': the great distinction is that Alfred wished to be remembered not by his notable deeds in war but by his 'good works' in peace.

THE LAST AGE OF SAXON ENGLAND

The tenth century saw England become for the first time a united kingdom. The Viking settlers in the Danelaw were conquered by the House of Wessex, and at the same time turned into Englishmen by conversion to Christianity and by their own willingness to fit into the life around them. Differences of law and custom persisted, and some peculiarities of speech; but after a couple of generations they no longer thought of themselves, or were regarded by the English, as foreign intruders.

The Danish lands were fitted into the shire system, which now (except in the North-West) assumed much the form it keeps today. The English half of Mercia had been organised into units round a central borough during the period of war and reconquest, and the Danes had themselves done the same with their half. The Kingdom of York remained as Yorkshire, but since it was far larger than other counties it was divided for practical purposes into thirds or 'ridings'. The remaining fragment of English Northumbria survived as Northumberland, though now far from the Humber, later to be still further reduced when its

northern part went to Scotland in 1018 and its southern became, in Norman times, the separate county palatine of the Bishops of Durham.

The forty years between the final submission of the Danelaw and the beginning of the Second Danish Wars is commonly regarded as the 'golden age' of Saxon England. It saw the great revival of monasteries associated with the name of Dunstan, and the recovery of the Church from the smashing blows which it had suffered at Viking hands. A century of laxity and decay, followed by destruction of buildings and slaughter or enslavement of inmates, had nearly wiped out monasteries throughout the kingdom; and Alfred's efforts to restart them had come to little because he simply could not find suitable men. Even ancient and renowned centres like Glastonbury only housed a shrunken body of clerics no longer living by the Rule.

Dunstan (c.910–988) was the son of a Somerset thegn, and born near Glastonbury himself. In his youth he attended the school there, and then, by the influence of an uncle who was Archbishop of Canterbury, he was introduced to King Athelstan's court. Here eventually he decided to take the monastic vows and priest's orders; and Athelstan's successor Edmund, in return for services, in 940 made him Abbot of what was left of Glastonbury. Here he set to work with a will, and during his fifteen years abbacy turned the place into the first genuine and regular English monastery for a century. Monks he trained were promoted to control and revive other houses, and spread the influence of his reform across the country. The detestable adolescent Ead-

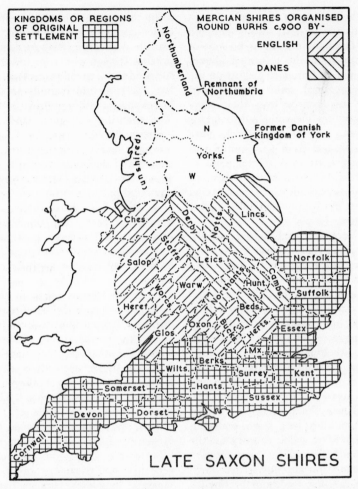

KINGDOMS OR REGIONS OF ORIGINAL SETTLEMENT

MERCIAN SHIRES ORGANISED ROUND BURHS c.900 BY-

ENGLISH

DANES

Northumberland

Remnant of Northumbria

Former Danish Kingdom of York

N

Yorks.

E

W

(unshired)

Ches.

Derby

Stafs

Notts.

Lincs.

Salop

Leics.

Norfolk

Worcs.

Warw

Northants.

Hunt.

Cambs.

Suffolk

Heref.

Beds.

Oxon

Bucks.

Herts.

Essex

Glos.

Mx.

Berks.

Wilts.

Surrey

Kent

Somerset

Hants.

Sussex

Devon

Dorset

Cornwall

LATE SAXON SHIRES

wig exiled him in 956, and for three years he lived in the great Benedictine abbey of St. Peter at Ghent in Flanders, where he learned of the great movement of monastic reform then centred on the French abbey of Clugny. Edgar in 959 recalled him, and soon made him Archbishop of Canterbury.

By this time Dunstan's pupils were everywhere in positions of authority, as bishops as well as abbots, and with the help of monks from France there was a widespread purge and reform of English houses. Edgar himself used the royal authority to back the movement. In the Danelaw, where there had been something like a clean sweep a century before, historic foundations like Ely, Thorney,

63

and Peterborough were restored.

The effect was felt throughout the Church. The appointment as bishops of monks trained in the reformed abbeys brought the new influence to bear on the parish clergy, and some much-needed discipline was exerted over their easy-going way of life. The sudden demand for service-books and religious works gave rise to the production of great numbers of finely copied Latin manuscripts, many of which were exported; and English bishops and missionaries of the new school played a large part in the conversion of Norway and Sweden.

At the accession of Ethelred, in 978, Saxon England had reached the peak of its achievement. Peace, unity, and strong government had transformed it from the chaotic conditions which Alfred had had to face a century before. But everything still hinged, in the last resort, on the king: and the fine record of Egbert's line ceased abruptly. Ethelred's weakness, untrustworthiness, and incompetence left the kingdom a prey to treachery within and renewed invasion from without. The Second Danish Wars, occupying almost all this regrettably long reign, ended in the conquest of the whole country and the rule of Cnut.* Though little immigration resulted, and Cnut speedily settled down to rule in the best traditions of English kingship, irreparable damage was done to the freedom and welfare of many Englishmen.

It is clear that there was fast developing, for a variety of reasons and in haphazard fashion, the arrangement that later times were to know as feudalism. We have seen the occasional necessity for

*See *The Vikings*, by R. R. Sellman.

a free man to put himself and his land under the protection of a lord, and the Danish Wars immensely speeded up the process. Ravaging of crops and stock, and the need for personal protection, played a large part: so did inability to meet the increasingly crushing burden of taxation. The granting of much land, free of ordinary public levies, for Church endowment had increased the strain on the rest; and Ethelred's enormous and frequent cash Danegeld taxes left many with no option but to give up their freedom to a wealthy man who would meet the burden for them. By late Saxon times very many, and probably most, previously free families were bound to a lord and holding their land on condition of labour service.

As many freemen sank in the social scale, so a few powerful families rose. The distance between king and ceorl was increased by the appearance of a new upper level of the aristocracy, far superior to the ordinary thegn and often themselves commanding the direct allegiance of a large section of the thegnhood. This was a sinister development, since in conditions of weak kingship it threatened the very existence of the realm. The reign of Edward the Confessor saw something very like the re-emergence of the old separate kingdoms, under Earls who might themselves be stronger than the king. In 1052 Earl Godwine of Wessex was able to return unbidden from exile, gather support from the seamen of the south-east ports, and force terms on the king himself. The danger was either that the king might become a mere figurehead, as in France, or that the royal line might be displaced entirely by that of one of the

EARLDOMS IN 1065

Sons of Godwine shaded

MORCAR

YORK

CHESTER

LINCOLN

EDWIN

GYRTH

WALTHEOF

HEREFORD

LEOFWINE

LONDON

HAROLD

WINCHESTER

powerful earls. In the latter case there was a chance of civil war, and more than a chance of disunity in the face of the enemy. In the event, it was the unwillingness of the northern earls to support Harold Godwineson in 1066 that allowed the Normans such a rapid and sweeping conquest.

CONCLUSION

The six centuries of the 'Anglo-Saxon period' saw the foundations of the English nation well and truly laid. Between the first settlements and the Norman Conquest stretched a period of time as long as that between ourselves and the Black Death—two-fifths of the entire history of the English in England. Century after century the unrecorded toil of pioneers cleared forest and broke new land to plough, until nearly every place on the modern map had its Saxon settlers. The open-field farming which they introduced to most of England remained typical till the enclosure movements of modern times. Gradually, out of internal struggle and foreign invasion, a united England emerged with almost the same boundaries (apart from Wales) as it has today. Law, administration, and government developed forms still firmly embedded in English institutions. Christianity, with its deep effects on English life, took root; and the parish system assumed the form, and often the same boundaries, that we now know.

There may be little visible in modern England that our Saxon forebears would recognise. The increasing tempo of change, especially in the last two centuries, has obliterated much of the landscape they knew and has given us, besides sprawling towns and industries, a countryside of hedged fields and separate farms. But beneath the surface there is still much in us and our ways of thinking and doing that goes back deep into our Saxon past. The roots are no less vital for being underground.

1066

A SELECT BOOK LIST

By Elizabeth N. Bewick, a.l.a.

The Anglo-Saxon Chronicle; translated and edited by G. N. Garmonsway. Dent (Everyman), 2nd edn., 1953. Booklist. A new translation presenting, in compact form, all the vernacular chronicles from the time of the arrival of the English to the year 1154.

Anglo-Saxon England. B.B.C., 1957. Illus., maps, booklist. Originally produced in conjunction with a series of broadcasts, this brief but informative pamphlet covers all aspects of Anglo-Saxon civilization, with many illustrations, a list of definitions and a table of comparative dates, and would be very useful as an outline for project work.

Bede's ecclesiastical history of the English nation; translated by John Stevens and revised by L. C. Jane. Dent (Everyman), repr. 1954. The story of the growth of the Christian religion in England up to A.D. 731.

BLAIR, PETER HUNTER. *An introduction to Anglo-Saxon England.* C.U.P., 1956. Illus., maps, booklist. A general introduction to the history of England between the Roman occupation and the Norman conquest, dealing particularly with the unification of the kingdom, the development of the English language and the growth of the Christian Church in England. Advanced.

BUNT, CYRIL. *Journeys through our early history.* 8 vols. Bruce, 1955. Illus., maps. An account of an imaginary journey through Britain and Ireland about the year 966, giving a picture of the everyday lives of the people, their manners, customs and beliefs. The volumes in the series cover Cambria, Northumbria, Caledonia, Ireland, Essex, East Anglia, Wessex and Mercia, and London.

DUCKETT, ELEANOR. *Alfred the Great and his England.* Collins, 1957. Maps, booklist. A detailed study of the life and times of King Alfred.

GORDON, R. K., ed. *Anglo-Saxon poetry.* Dent (Everyman), rev. edn. 1954. English poetry between A.D. 650 and 1000 from "Widsith" and "Beowulf" to the battle-pieces of "Brunanburh" and "Maldon".

HODGKIN, R. H. *A history of the Anglo-Saxons.* 2 vols. O.U.P., 3rd edn., 1953. Illus., maps. A history of the Angles and Saxons to the time of the death of Alfred. A detailed and expensive work of reference invaluable to the serious student.

OMAN, SIR CHARLES. *England before the Norman Conquest.* (History of England, Vol. 1.) Methuen, 9th edn., 1949. Maps. Covers the Celtic, Roman and Anglo-Saxon periods, down to 1066.

QUENNELL, MARJORIE AND C. H. B. *Everyday life in Anglo-Saxon, Viking and Norman times.* Batsford, 4th edn., 1955. Illus., booklist. Covers the Anglo-Saxon period from the social aspect, the people and how they lived, their character, dress, houses, education and literature, with a chronological time-chart of events.

STENTON, SIR FRANK M. *Anglo-Saxon England.* (Oxford History of England, Vol. 2.) O.U.P., 2nd edn., 1947. Maps, booklist. The standard work of reference on the period for the advanced student, covering religious, political and social history from the emergence of the first English kingdoms to the death of William the Conqueror; with a full bibliography.

WHITELOCK, DOROTHY. *The beginnings of English society.* Penguin Books, 1952. Booklist. Describes the English way of life from the middle of the fifth century to the Norman conquest, particularly noting the effect of the spread of Christianity and the art and literature which it inspired.

English historical documents. Eyre & Spottiswoode, 1955. Gives texts of the more important of the contemporary sources for Anglo-Saxon history up to 1042.

INDEX

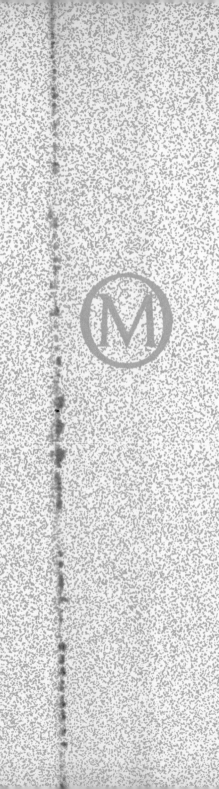